The Rough Guide to

Saving & Selling Online

1st edition

ROUGH
GUIDES

www.roughguides.com

Credits

**The Rough Guide to
Saving & Selling Online**

Editor: Peter Buckley
Design and layout: Peter Buckley & Andrew Clare
Proofreading: Jason Freeman
Production: Rebecca Short & Vicky van der Luit

Rough Guides Reference

Director: Andrew Lockett
Editors: Kate Berens, Peter Buckley,
Tracy Hopkins, Matthew Milton,
Joe Staines, Ruth Tidball

Publishing information

This first edition published January 2010 by
Rough Guides Ltd, 80 Strand, London, WC2R 0RL
Email: mail@roughguides.com

Distributed by the Penguin Group:
Penguin Books Ltd, 80 Strand, London, WC2R 0RL
Penguin Group (USA), 375 Hudson Street, NY 10014, USA
Penguin Group (Australia), 250 Camberwell Road, Camberwell, Victoria 3124, Australia
Penguin Group (Canada), 90 Eglinton Avenue East, Suite 700, Toronto, Ontario, Canada M4P 2Y3
Penguin Group (New Zealand), Cnr Rosedale and Airborne Roads, Albany, Auckland, New Zealand

Printed and bound in Singapore by Toppan Security Printing Pte Ltd

Typeset in Calibri, Minion and Myriad to an original design by Peter Buckley

Front cover image © GK Hart/Vikki Hart

224 pages; includes index

A catalogue record for this book is available from the British Library.

ISBN 13: 978-1-84836-519-3

1   3   5   7   9   8   6   4   2

The Rough Guide to

Saving & Selling Online

Ian Peel

www.roughguides.com

Contents

About This Book

If you want to live a cheaper, leaner, more frugal life, then the Internet will guide you. This book roots out several hundred websites, blogs, portals and services to help you really make the most of your finances.

If you want to make some money by selling online, eBay is the classic destination. And this book tells you pretty much everything you need to know to sell high and buy low. There are a host of other websites – not least Amazon Marketplace – that outshine eBay in some respects, so we cover those too.

To save money, you need to delve into the world of comparison sites. The whole process – and comparison sites for all manner of goods – are examined. We look at Freecycling, and stacks of websites to save you money in general life, whether it's on travel, phone calls, house hunting, and so on. From tips on downloading vouchers and discount codes, to websites for reclaiming bank charges, this book will save you money. I hope to take you on a journey to circumnavigate the big sell and the big fees that traditional high street stores and banks rely upon.

Ian Peel

Acknowledgements

Thanks to Peter Buckley and the Rough Guides team, and to everyone that chipped in with ideas along the way. For my family.

Part 1: FAQs

1

FAQs #1: Sites For Saving Money

Everything You Were Afraid To Ask...

Hold on a minute, before we get started, what exactly is an FAQ?

An FAQ is just retro Internet terminology for the phrase "Frequently Asked Questions". You might call it a Q&A section. Or alternatively just a preface.

Great, so why a book about selling stuff and making savings using the Internet?

The whole point of this book is frugal living – making the most of what you've got. On the one hand that means using the Internet to make money, by selling off the stuff you don't need. And, on the other, it's about the various websites you can use to help get the things you need to buy at the best possible price.

What exactly do you mean by saving money?

Good question for the start of an FAQ! Yes, saving money could mean, on the one hand, savings accounts, online banking, and maximizing your interest rates. On the other hand, it means paying less for your purchases, price reductions and discounts. That's the sort of saving money we're talking about here.

OK. Well everyone knows shopping online is generally cheaper than in "real life" stores. So there's not much more to say is there?

There's lots to say. Firstly there's the fact that the Internet opens up a whole world of choice. Not everything is cheaper on sites like **eBay** and **Amazon**, and we've packed the relevant chapters of this book to help you buy what you want for the cheapest price.

What other ways can I use my Internet connection to help save money?

Plenty, and this is where the "tips and tricks" parts of many of the chapters in this book come into play. A great example is **SAYNOTO0870.com**, a UK website that provides standard landline-rate phone numbers as alternatives to premium rate enquiry lines. The site is free to use and is guaranteed to decrease your monthly phone bill.

Can't I just Google this site and others like it?

You could but, for starters, you need to know that the site exists in the first place. Which is where this *Rough Guide* comes in. And secondly, these sites need to be found, tested and tried out, before being recommended. This isn't a phone book-style directory, it's the result of putting word-of-mouth recommendations for sites to the test.

But there's never such a thing as a free lunch is there?

Actually, sometimes there is. A lot of the comparison sites thrive because they pipe adverts to you as you shop and browse. If you can put up with that, then you're harnessing all of their power for nothing. And some of the self-help websites (like the aforementioned **Saynotto0870.com**, or the famous eBay

search tool **FatFingers.com**) are set up by willing volunteers with nothing more than a good idea and some online community spirit behind them.

What areas of daily life are we talking about here?

We think you can use the Internet to make major savings on all areas of daily life. This is why we've set this book out as it is: full chapters on all the monster sites for selling your stuff and making savings – not just Amazon Marketplace and eBay, but also the UK's notorious **MoneySavingExpert.com** (see p.176), and classifieds sites like **Gumtree** (see p.92) and **Craigslist** (see p.89). We've also included chapters on different areas of daily life: travel (see p.144), technology (see p.157), domestic finance (see p.175) and so on.

Doesn't that add up to a lot of reading before I can get online and start saving?

Not at all – this is a guide that you can dip into whenever you need it. For example the next time you buy your car insurance or book a flight, make sure you've tried all the sites we suggest to help get the best deals.

Sounds great, but isn't this all a little bit, you know, cheapskate?

Quite the reverse. It's all coming from a post-excess, recession-specific ideology. Exactly what **Timothy Leary** meant when he said "Just Say Know". After all, there are corporate meetings taking place every hour of every day, in which companies large and small think of new ways to get us to part with the most amount of cash for the least amount in return. This book is here to balance the scales and give you the most return for the least expense. As are self-help websites like **Frugalliving.About.com** and the various others explored in these pages.

Chapter 1

I get it. It's all about "frugality" rather than "cheapskatedness", right?

Exactly. Farhad Manjoo from *Slate, The Washington Post*'s daily webzine, hit the nail on the head in a piece entitled "The Frugal Life" (slate.com/id/2207305). "The frugality cult emphasizes that their lifestyle is different from merely being cheap", he says. "Eating at McDonald's is cheap. Cooking dinner and saving the leftovers for lunch the next day is frugal."

What kind of savings are there to be had?

That varies wildly depending on what you're shopping for of course. But **CDs and books** can generally be found on the likes of **Amazon Marketplace** and **Half.com** for around fifty percent of their high-street prices. And – at the higher end of spending – you might save a small percentage of your house move costs if you really shop around with the sites in that particular chapter. Many frugal livers tackled the economic downturn by aiming to shave ten percent off their monthly outgoings, and have succeeded with no noticeable downturn in quality of life. That has to be a good target to aim for!

So who are you, how did you get into this, and are you some kind of frugal living cult leader?

Nope – nothing as scary as that. I'm a journalist and I've been writing about the Internet since 1992 – a couple of years before the World Wide Web was invented. In the late 1990s I found a job I liked and an employer that treated me well. But by the late 2000s, I came to the classic realization – that I'd slogged for ten years making money for other people rather than for myself. So just as the credit crunch was turning into full-blown recession, I had a *Prisoner* moment and resigned. Funnily enough the first and most scary thing I had to get my head around wasn't how to earn money but how to save it. Earning money is never that tricky – earning *enough* is the tricky thing. And it gets easier if you reduce your overheads. Which was the next big challenge...

So what did you do?

I asked around. I'd spent years being what you might call "comfortably salaried" – not earning a mint by any means but having enough to pay the bills and not worry too much and now I was starting again from scratch, ground zero for the bank account. But with all the hang-ups of someone with a regular salary: car insurance organized for speed not value, TV and phone suppliers that had never been shopped around for or weighed up, and so on. I got the best advice of all from my brother – within minutes he jumped online,

got a spreadsheet of my outgoings sorted (using a version of **Vertex 24**'s free Personal Budget Spreadsheet for Excel, vertex42.com/ExcelTemplates/personal-budget-spreadsheet.html), checked one website to value my car (parkers.co.uk, ready to sell it!) and looked up another that showed me I was overpaying for my broadband connection by about £20 per month (ukbroadbandguide.com)! I knew his advice would be good too, because he's the only person I've ever met who's **paid off his mortgage early**! (This one's for you Ken-lad!) So *Slate*'s "cult of frugality" really appealed to me, and it's an attitude that's growing. I soon decided that frugality is like 1970s self-sufficiency and 1960s hippydom with a twist of 1990s "cyberspace" excitement. And about time too, given the every-man-for-themselves 1980s and dot.com/dot.bomb 1990s.

OK, enough questions already. But the last one's the most important. Do you practice what you preach?

Well I'm writing this very sentence using **Open Office** (openoffice.org), a completely free – and somewhat better specified – alternative to Microsoft Word, produced by **Sun Microsystems**. I'm paying for my broadband connection as I do so, but earlier today (honest) I made sure I was not overpaying for it by checking the latest on the blogs at **Broadbandsuppliers.co.uk**. Oh,

Chapter 1

and I'm surfing the net with another free alternative to Microsoft: Google's very fast **Chrome** browser. As I do so I'm listening to a brilliant live session by Little Boots (littlebootsmusic.co.uk) on BBC Radio 1 through my PC using the **BBC iPlayer** (bbc.co.uk/iplayer). And, according to Ashley Highfield, the BBC's Director of Future Media and Technology, you don't need to buy a TV licence to enjoy such BBC TV or radio programmes on your PC. At least not for now... Read more in his blog "iPlayer Doesn't Require a TV Licence... Yet" at bbc.co.uk/blogs/bbcinternet/2008/01/iplayer_does_not_require_a_tv_1.html.

2

FAQs #2: Sites For Selling

Everything Else You Were Afraid To Ask...

So, which are the good websites to help me sell my stuff?

All will become clear in the ensuing chapters, but by far the most popular are **eBay** and **Amazon**. eBay, for example, by the time of its tenth birthday in 2005 had attracted 181 million users, buying and selling across 33 countries. Between them they had traded goods in that year alone totalling over $44 billion. There is also a whole host of lesser-known sites, some of which certainly have their merits.

What are these lesser-known sites?

We'll devote a whole chapter to them later, but they include **Play.com**'s version of **Amazon Marketplace**, **PlayTrade**, eBay-wannabes like **Auctions United**, and the second-hand marketplace **Preloved**.

Chapter 2

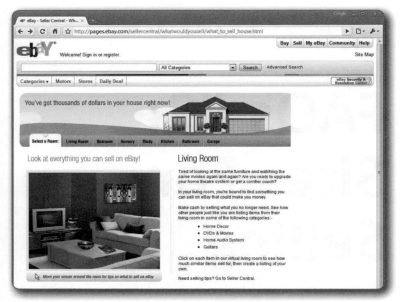

Great, I need some extra cash at the moment. How can I get some ideas on what to sell?

You can find an interactive house to tour around, clicking into virtual rooms to find inspiration for what you might sell, in eBay's **Seller Central** department. Like most of its smaller seller tools, it's hidden way down in an obscure corner of the site, but can be found by going direct to pages.ebay.com/sellercentral/whatwouldyousell/what_to_sell_house.html. Or, if you plan to clear out your wardrobe, Lisa Thompson's **Fortunes From Fashion** newsletter is well worth a look. You can view a couple of recent issues for free at fortunesfromfashion.com/Public_Pages/Sales_Info/Sample_Issues.

Do I really have anything worth selling?

You may not be sitting on an untapped gold mine, but you could be sitting on a few month's wages, if statistics from market research agency **AC Neilson** are anything to go by. The average American household has approximately $2200 worth of unused items that could be sold on eBay, they say, having surveyed two thousand homes. Besides, if you really don't think you have anything that will sell, you could still experiment. "Retired banker Arden Peterson, 62, let

Watch Your Language

You may not be multilingual but there are a couple of handy Web-tools to allow you to add some international flavour to your sales listings. The classic is Babel Fish (babelfish.altavista.com). You type in your words, and it throws them back in the language of your choice. Google also has its own language tools at google. com/language_tools and for exchange rates there's the perennially handy xe.net/ucc Universal Currency Converter.

his son Mitch, an **iSold It** trading assistant put a 1929 $10 bank note from his collection on eBay just for fun", reported *Time*'s Sally Stitch in November 2005, "but also because a very rare 1905 $10 bank note had sold on eBay a month earlier for $27,000. The fun turned serious when Peterson's bank note fetched $1,037…"

Stella Klainman, founder of the **FoundValue** chain of eBay drop-off shops, has seen a massive rise in recent years in the number of digital cameras being sold on eBay because, as she told **AuctionBytes.com**, "the technology is steadily improving while prices are dropping, leading many shoppers to eBay in search of newer models at bargain prices." If you plan to upgrade your camera, her tip-list for selling your old one can be found at auctionbytes.com/cab/abu/y206/m03/abu0163/s03.

What kind of stuff will be popular with buyers?

Head to eBay's **Pulse section** (at pulse.ebay.com, or pulse.ebay.co.uk in the UK), which provides a straightforward snapshot of what's popular and what's selling well. Anything Wii- or *High School Musical*-related is selling very well on eBay at the moment, as this book goes to press. From the main Pulse page you can access popularity charts on everything from antiques to baby goods (both very busy areas of trade) which might give you some ideas for what you could sell and how much money you could raise. A few years back, when we put together *The Rough Guide to eBay*, the top ten was dominated by the iPod, Xbox 360, PSP, Louis Vuitton and *Star Wars*.

From the main Pulse page you can access similar pages for the 35 main categories. So, the most popular searches in **Dolls & Bears**? Barbie, of course. And in **Antiques**? Furniture: Victorian and French.

How difficult will it be to sell my stuff online?

When eBay launched in 1995, it wasn't the easiest system to navigate. Even five years ago, it was popular only with those online all day at work, and even then only for buying and selling small, easily postable goods. But with the growth of broadband and the boom in online shopping in general, eBay and its competitors can be – and are – used by anyone and everyone.

And you'll be in good company – eBay's famous users are just as varied as the products they shop for, and include **Cherie Blair** (spotted buying toys for her kids, and shoes for herself), **Damon Albarn** (spotted selling his sofa), **Jennifer Garner** (buying an antique barber's chair), **Gordon Ramsay** (selling off a car registration plate), **Eva Longoria** (searching for a premium Xbox 360 for her boyfriend), **Robbie Williams** (selling his bread maker), **Katie Holmes** (collecting rare books), designer **Wayne Hemingway** ("I treat it like going to a jumble sale, I look for things that make me smile", he says), **Nicky Hilton** (buying Marilyn Monroe photos for sister Paris), **Girls Aloud** (regular eBay clothes shoppers), and **Jemima Khan** and **Jessica Simpson** (both buying clothes, though not together).

What about online auctions – should I put stuff under the hammer or sell it for a fixed price?

While most second-hand sites like Amazon allow you to set the price you want to sell at, eBay, of course, is renowned for its auction system. There are various different types, too (a normal auction, reserve price, Dutch, private and so on). If you can, it's best to test out a few of the systems on smaller price items, to get a feel for how buyers react. If the item you want to sell is a one-off, try an auction listing.

If you have several identical items, try a **fixed-price** site, or the fixed-price system on eBay which is called Buy It Now (pages.ebay.com/services/buyandsell/buyitnow-overview.html). If, on the other hand, you have a one-off item to auction but you're as interested in getting quick results as you are the final fee, then try an auction with a built-in **Buy It Now**. This allows people to bid from your starting price, but you've also set a fixed price point you'd be happy to sell at, should someone want to steam in and take the goods straight off your hands.

Auctions can often yield higher profit, but are riskier. Fixed-price sites and Buy It Now may make you less money but there's also less chance of making no money at all. There's a useful chart in eBay's Help section that compares the costs and benefits of the main listing types from a seller's perspective at **Help > Selling > Listing Your Item > Selecting a Selling Format**.

If you're looking to sell quickly, it's a fact that Buy It Now speeds up the process. Which is probably why it accounts for over one third of all sales. "While auctions run for an average of seven days, items sold via Buy It Now

Unpaid Item Process

Remember that on eBay you must file your unpaid item dispute within 45 days of an auction closing, and work quickly while eBay tries to get you in touch with the buyer. If the dispute isn't resolved within sixty days, eBay moves on, files it as a lost cause and you lose your rights to a refund. Your only recourse for a non-paying buyer at that stage is to leave them negative feedback, which you're quite within your rights to do. In the Help section, go to **Transaction Problems and Protections > Protection for Sellers > Unpaid Item Process** to report a rogue buyer. Another way to cover your costs if it all goes pear-shaped is the **Second Chance Offer** system. Since November of 2005 there's been a link to this from the **Dispute Closed** pages, allowing you to get in touch with the second highest bidder and offer them a chance to buy the item instead.

All of this advice applies to buyers who don't pay while you wait to ship their item. But what about buyers who you ship to, but then refuse to pay up, maybe adding insult to injury by claiming that the goods never arrived? The obvious answer is to never ship goods until monies have been received, although this isn't always possible, especially as there are some known flaws in the PayPal system that allow spurious buyers to exploit sellers, taking their goods and even their money.

Paypalsucks.com points to a number of cases where buyers will accept goods, sometimes even thanking the seller and confirming receipt, but then complain to their credit card company that they hadn't received anything. The credit card company issues a "chargeback" to PayPal, recovering the buyer's funds and leaving the unwitting seller in the red. It can happen easily, and PayPal admit that they are relatively powerless to resist chargebacks from credit card companies, a spokesperson telling the UK site **This Is Money** that, if a chargeback is issued, "PayPal will fight the case on the seller's behalf but in most cases the card issuer will demand the money back." Hence the warning tucked away on the PayPal site, that it "reserves the right not to dispute a chargeback

even if the seller has provided some evidence, particularly if PayPal believes the dispute is not likely to be successful." Which, in plain English, means that even if you can prove that the seller received the goods, PayPal can still go along with the chargeback and leave you out of pocket.

Reserve Price Auctions – Best Avoided

It's worth noting that a reserve price on an auction can often scare bidders off just as much as an overly ambitious starting price. If you put yourself in the buyer's shoes, they can be very frustrating. You bid once and get rejected. You bid again, and are again rejected. All because of a secret reserve price which, a buyer might assume after a couple of failed attempts, is way out of their price range. So they move on to someone else's auction and leave yours behind. This is why most eBay sellers not only use reserve prices very judiciously, but they'll also go as far as including "No Reserve!" in the headline or listing. As eBay itself says in the Best Practices section, "statistics show [although they're cagey as to what the exact numbers are] that items listed *without* a reserve usually sell for more than comparable items listed *with* a reserve."

turn over in an average of less than three days", reports *Forbes* magazine.

How much is it going to cost me to set up and start selling?

Nothing. To start browsing, buying and selling, you just need to be sitting at an Internet-connected computer. For now, for the uninitiated, remember that eBay and similar sites are – all hype aside – just websites. Unlike other Internet phenomena like **iTunes** or **Google Earth**, you won't need to download, install or configure any software. All you need is some time, a Web browser and you're up and running.

How much money might I make?

There's good money to be made by selling all sorts of second-hand goods online. Outside of the examples you'll find in this book there's a thriving community of sellers willing to share their experiences. A case in point is a blogger and online seller called Cady from Gulfport, Florida, who writes her own *Fiscal Fitness* journal on the brilliantly titled **Get Rich Slowly** website (getrichslowly.org). One of her articles covers a massive clear-out of CDs, having decided to try and sell anything she hadn't listened to in a year.

Adults Only

Selling online is for adults only. Amazon doesn't state a minimum age, saying only that "minors are not allowed to use (its) services" and that "use of the site and services is limited to parties that lawfully can enter into and form contracts under applicable law." eBay, on the other hand, states that it is for over-eighteens only. That said, if you're under age and want to join the millions of others using the system you should have a parent or guardian register and use their account under supervision. Otherwise you will be on very shaky ground should legal action ever be taken against (or for) you in regards to items bought or sold.

"Although I'm losing in double-digits percentage-wise on (Amazon) commission, fees and shipping", she reports, "I've gained about $160 I didn't have otherwise. Those discs were just sitting there, and I'd have had to put out quite a bit of effort without using Amazon to turn that stack of 28 CDs into $160. I wouldn't have made $6 per disc at a yard sale. I've tried visiting local used CD shops and I get maybe $1 a disc if I'm lucky." You can read her full story at getrichslowly.org/blog/2007/09/23/how-to-use-the-amazon-marketplace-for-fun-and-profit (and see the mountain of music she was tackling on Flickr at flickr.com/photos/firepile/50821898).

What do I need to be able to take orders?
This is the beauty of selling online through the major websites – you don't need to worry about setting up special accounts to take people's credit or debit card details. They handle all of that for you. The only thing you might want to set up – if you don't have one already – is a **PayPal** account, which is by far the most popular person-to-person online payment method.

It's quite straightforward to set up an account with PayPal and they also offer an easy workaround to allow you to accept credit card payments without too much hassle or outlay. In the past, accepting credit cards online was one big headache and certainly not for home sellers. Accepting credit card payments with PayPal costs nothing to set up, you just have to hand over 2.2 percent on each transaction. The trouble is, not everyone knows this is actually possible. So in order to attract people to your online or eBay sales you need to make it very graphically visible in your listing or classified ad that, yes, they can pay you by credit card and, yes,

clicking your PayPal logo will allow them to do so! You can get all the logos and source code you'll need from paypal.com.

Can I sell to anyone, anywhere in the world?

Well, through Amazon and eBay alone you'll have a pool of prospective buyers in hundreds of countries at your fingertips. In fact it would be crazy to think that – unlike the world of the newspaper ad – the items you sell are going to be bought by someone living nearby. Furthermore, if your items are relatively light and un-bulky, but high in value, then they'll be an attractive proposition to buyers the world over. So before you go ahead and click "submit" on your sales listing, consider where you can and can't ship to. Take a look at websites like **USPS** (usps.com) for mailing from the US and the **Post Office** (royalmail.com) in the UK to get an idea of how much extra you'll need to charge if your buyer turns out to be in Austria, Angola, or wherever.

On **Amazon**, you have on offer a simple set of choices of where on the planet you can tell your buyers you'll ship to. On **eBay**, you can select your "Ship-to locations" when you complete the Sell Your Item form. You can also choose to have eBay's own **International Shipping Calculator** added into your listing so browsers can see for themselves how much extra they should expect to pay.

What about – gulp – paying tax on all this?

In the UK, there's a threshold which few home traders exceed. £5435 is the magic number. If you don't exceed this in earnings on top of your full-time job, if you have one, then you don't need to worry about tax.

If you do exceed this figure, or are self-employed, then head to **HM Revenue & Customs** for a surprisingly straightforward guide to what you need to do. It's here: hmrc.gov.uk/sa. And for an independent guide to the tax issue for online sellers in the UK, check out **Moneymagpie**'s 2009 feature at moneymagpie. com/article/713/making-extra-money-do-i-have-to-pay-extra-tax.

In the US it's a roughly similar story. If you're selling your own secondhand goods online you don't need to worry about tax because, in theory, you're not making a profit (assuming you sell something for less than what you paid for it new). Try the interactive, discussion-based article on the subject on **Moolanomy** (moolanomy.com/1126/do-you-have-to-pay-taxes-selling-on-ebay), which is jargon-free and populated by like-minded traders as opposed to financial "gurus". There's also a useful guide to tax – what it is and why and how you pay – at the business directory **QCK** (qck.com/personal-tax-guide.html).

If you're planning on setting up a business online, the golden rule is to get accurate accounts running from the outset. "One of the main reasons small businesses fail is they don't seek legal and accounting help at the beginning", eBay PowerSeller Patrick Snetsinger told Janelle Elms for business website **MSNBC.com**. So monitor and keep evidence of all sales made, fees paid (to eBay and PayPal) and all assets bought. Whatever tax you end up having to pay, keeping these records will make sure it's fair, and as painless as possible.

In the US matters are sometimes complicated by tax laws which vary from state to state. So anyone running an online business should appoint a local, qualified professional to handle legal and accounting affairs. They'll have to be on the ball too, because as quickly as the Internet evolves, so do the tax implications. The bottom line? "You need to decide if this is a business, a hobby, or you're just selling off collectibles", as Eva Rosenberg of **TaxMama.com** says in the *E-Commerce Times*, because "each choice has different tax effects. If you're a business, you must have a profit motive, with plans to make the business turn a profit."

What if buyers don't pay?

This is the worry of any online seller, and it's certainly not an unheard of occurrence. First things first – **how long to wait** for someone to pay? Sellers are often itching to get their money, and start worrying if they haven't heard from their buyer after a couple of days. Amazon Marketplace sellers are fine, as buyers pay up on the spot, as soon as they say "yes please" to an item. But eBay's rule-of-thumb is to stay cool for seven days. Give the buyer time to get in touch and sort out and, if necessary, mail their money. If you've still heard nothing after seven days – or if they did pay but the cheque bounced – then you need to get your head around the **Unpaid Item Process**. This is where eBay starts by sending an email and pop-up message to your buyer to remind them to pay. If they fail to do so, you can get a refund on your listing fee and can relist the item for nothing.

Could I get someone to do all this for me?

You could, but it would reduce your profits. Selling online can certainly make you money but it can also be time-consuming and fiddly. Photography, form filling, difficult buyers, figuring postage rates, packaging up and posting items … and that's if it's a straightforward sale. You certainly have to be prepared to put the time in. As an alternative to doing it yourself, you might use one of many eBay drop-off centres or trading assistants, collectively known as **consignment sellers**.

Chapter 2

You give your goods to a trusted, reputable assistant or centre and they sell them on eBay for you, handling the entire process from end to end. You drop off your goods and pick up the cash – if they've sold – a week later. There's a price of course, and the standard commission is thirty per-cent. **eBay trading assistants** come in all shapes and sizes but it's not always that easy to find one. eBay has a handy search tool for finding your nearest assistant, but it's hidden away in the Sell section. You'll find it by going to **Seller Central > Advanced Selling > Trading Assistants**.

Drop-off centres are easier to find because they have physical shop-fronts. They've spread quickly in the US since the idea was first hatched in California in 2002. It's estimated that there are over ten thousand such stores in the US, while in the UK the idea has been much slower to take off. Here's the lowdown on the two different types of centre:

1 Basic eBay sales offices Although note that few are officially affiliated or endorsed. Like a bricks and mortar shop-front to the website itself, two popular ones are **Auctioning4U** (UK, auctioning4u.co.uk) and **iSold It** (US, i-soldit.com).

2 Consultants These guys take on high-value items like classic cars and antiques. You don't drop off; they come to you to photograph and value the item, a job done by the likes of the UK's **SellStuffEasy** (sellstuffeasy.com).

I like this FAQ approach. Where can I read more questions and answers?

Two great places to start are the self-help, **Q&A** sites **Google Answers** (answers.google.com) and **Yahoo! Answers** (answers.yahoo.com), both of which regularly have chatter on all aspects of selling online. On **Amazon**, click on **Sell Your Stuff** from the home page, then click **Learn more and sign up** and you'll find their own FAQ. **eBay** has its own FAQs too, of course – just click the **Help** link at the top of the home page. But for independent answers, compiled by users themselves, check the rather cumbersome URL of faqs.org/faqs/business/online-marketing/ebay, which is the work of the alt.marketing.online.ebay forum.

Part 2: eBay Vs Amazon

3

Buying On eBay

Dipping Into The Global Bargain Bin

Massive choice? Definitely. Bargain prices? Possibly. *And* the addictive fun of bidding at auction. These are the three main reasons people buy via eBay and online auctions. Millions of items from around the world and, for second-hand goods, often starting at barmy prices. Not surprisingly,

 anything small and easy to mail is a particularly popular buy – so you'll find masses of choice on eBay if you collect toy cars, or want to improve your CD collection.

But you can in theory buy almost anything of any shape or size. A left shoe by an obscure Japanese fashion house, to go with the right that became orphaned back in the 1980s? Or maybe you want to beat the High Street price on a new turntable? Chances are you can find it somewhere.

As eBay has expanded, so have the goods available, from **collectibles** to **furniture**, **cars** and even **houses**. Everyone thought eBay was crazy when their **eBayMotors.com** spin-off was launched in 2000, but now a new or used vehicle is bought every four minutes of every day...

Buying goods on eBay is quite simple. First, you find what you want – either by searching for something specific, or browsing the myriad of product categories. Most items will either be up for auction – usually for a seven-day period – or for sale at a fixed price (known as **Buy It Now**). For the latter, just click to buy and place your order as you would in any other online store. And eBay's auctions work just the same as those in "real life": you decide what you want to pay and place a bid.

Unlike a traditional auction though, eBay does some of the bidding for you. Having stated the maximum you'd like to pay, it bids incrementally on your behalf, based on a number of preset scales. Say you see some shoes with a current or starting bid of £10, and you're willing to pay up to £20. Place your bid of £20, and that will trigger the price to increase to £10.50. Between now and the end of the auction, anyone else will have to bid higher than £20 to be in the running. But if no one does, the shoes are yours for £10.50. This is called proxy bidding.

Buying on eBay differs from real life in another obvious but crucial way – it's effectively **blind**. You don't get to physically see either the goods you're bidding on or the person you're buying from. Can they be trusted, and are the goods for real? These are questions you should always have in the back of your mind, and we'll come on to specific checks. But for now, before you buy anything on eBay – or any online site – the first and most important thing to do is click around and get a feel for the place.

The Process

Bidding and buying goods on eBay is a simpler process than buying from many well-known online shops, but there are many traps to fall into if you don't watch out. First and foremost is **postage costs**. Always make sure you check these before you bid or buy. Sellers will often try and attract you with very cheap goods, but insist on high postage costs, to make sure they make a

Chapter 3

profit. They should list their shipping fees up front, but if they don't, just click the "Ask Seller a Question" link to find out where you stand.

Like any other purchase on or offline, you also need to carefully examine the seller's shipping insurance details and returns policy, both of which should be covered in the item listing. Unlike other shops though, on eBay these will vary from seller to seller, so don't forget to check them over every time you make a purchase.

If your mouse is still hovering excitedly over the "Place Bid" button, remember that clicking this enters you into a binding agreement with the seller. You are obliged to follow through the transaction, so only click that button if you're absolutely sure. From here on in it's very difficult to back out.

When you've made a bid you'll want to follow the progress of the auction. A simple way to do this is just to set your browser home page to the auction listing – that way you'll see who the highest bidder is and the price the item has reached every time you open your browser. But if you're bidding on or following more than one particular item, the **My eBay** portal is far more practical. If you get outbid you'll receive an email alert and a very unsubtle "don't let this item get away!" message encouraging you to bid again.

Try placing a few "practice" bids on low-price items to lose your eBay virginity. There's nothing like **first-hand experience** – best gained by buying a £2 CD rather than a £200 Rolex. There's also a Practice Bids section where you can click your way through an auction without having to part with any cash. Find it under **Help > Learning Centre > How To Buy**. Once you've carried out a few test auctions the proxy bidding system becomes rather more comfortable.

If there's a product you're really desperate for, there's a temptation to bid on every one available. This is another pitfall to avoid. If you win two auctions for the same item (albeit from different sellers) then you're obliged to pay for both. Another temptation is, having been outbid on one item, to immediately bid on something similar from another seller. But try and hold

Bid Increments

As eBay automatically does your bidding for you, based on the maximum price you're prepared to pay, it's useful to know the increments at which it will bid up. In other words the amount by which the price of an item will rise each time your bid is bettered by another user. You can find a full list at pages.ebay.co.uk/help/buy/bid-increments.html.

Shill Bidding: A Word Of Warning

Also known as shilling, scamming, bid padding or just plain old dirty tricks, this is where unscrupulous sellers get their friends or family – or even themselves under a separate eBay identity – to bid up their own items, artificially raising the price to get more money out of legitimate buyers. It happens often and is one of eBay's greatest weaknesses as it's very difficult to police. eBay recommends that family members, friends and people living with, working with or sharing a computer with a seller should not bid on their items. But this isn't monitored and it's very difficult to check yourself. Warning signs to look out for are if you're locked in an ever-escalating price war with one other bidder. Or if you lose out on the auction of a low-value item, only for the seller to contact you saying the winning bidder has pulled out. Both of these instances could also arise for perfectly legitimate reasons, too, of course.

off until the first auction has finished. The person that originally outbid you may cancel or retract, leaving you as the highest bidder or winner of the item you originally went after.

Feedback

eBay had been running for six months and closed almost ten thousand auctions by February 1996 at which point founder **Pierre Omidyar** single-handedly put together the **Feedback system**, a scorecard designed to sort the good users from the bad.

Feedback is often dressed up into some kind of philosophy. Even Omidyar refers to it as his "grand hope", designed to drive away and expose dishonest shoppers and sellers. And it's since been replicated on Amazon and all manner of competitor sites. It's also become an integral part of the eBay experience – and has decreased the aforementioned worry of buying and selling "blind". In fact, with members now having left billions of feedback comments about each other, it's become possibly the world's largest charter of "trust".

How does feedback work? Buyers and sellers leave one-line appraisals and a positive, negative or neutral score on each other, each time a transaction is completed. All the scores are added up to make a rating for every eBay user.

A user can only increase or decrease another's rating by one point no matter how many positive or negative experiences they've had, the theory

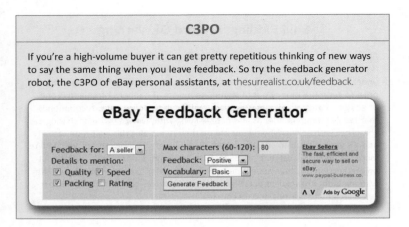

C3PO

If you're a high-volume buyer it can get pretty repetitious thinking of new ways to say the same thing when you leave feedback. So try the feedback generator robot, the C3PO of eBay personal assistants, at thesurrealist.co.uk/feedback.

eBay Feedback Generator

Feedback for: A seller

Details to mention:
☑ Quality ☑ Speed
☑ Packing ☐ Rating

Max characters (60-120): 80
Feedback: Positive
Vocabulary: Basic
Generate Feedback

being if you've had a bad experience with a seller, why would you want to buy from them again?

Feedback is the basis of the **Meet the Seller** panel you'll see at the top right of every item listing. You can see how they score and also read every individual feedback comment they've ever received. The higher the score listed after the seller's user ID the more positive feedback they've received.

As your score gets higher you start to move around eBay, wearing the equivalent of a McDonald's staff badge, with stars collected for good behaviour. A yellow star will appear next to your ID when you hit ten feedback points, a blue when you hit fifty points and so on – right up to a red shooting star when your feedback score hits one hundred thousand.

There are numerous opportunities to leave feedback when you've bought your item. You'll see links in your "Item Won!" confirmation email or go direct to the **Feedback Forum** at pages.ebay.com/services/forum/feedback. html. You'll also find that sellers will nag you to leave feedback for them. They need you to do so to increase their score and thus increase their earning potential. Like bidding, leaving a feedback comment is permanent. So consider if you really do want to tarnish a seller's reputation before you vent your spleen about late arriving goods…

While feedback is certainly useful, it shouldn't lull you into a false sense of security. If you're considering buying from a seller with a high feedback score, you should still check through their member profile to see what negative comments have been left for them. You might find, for example, that they

The Golden Rule

The essential feedback tip? Don't buy from sellers who have lots of negative feedback, or a low positive percentage, no matter how tempting they make their items sound. Feedback algebra for the mathematically challenged is explained in detail at pages.ebay.com/help/feedback/feedback-scores.html, and there's a detailed, if obvious, breakdown of the various elements of the **Seller Information** panel at pages.ebay.com/help/feedback/evaluating-feedback.html.

are generally very trustworthy but are particularly difficult to deal with if posting oversize items, or calculating international shipping. Member profiles can be kept private – so if you come across a seller that's chosen to do so, proceed with caution.

It's also best to be cautious of members who have changed their user ID. It *can* happen for a legitimate reason, but they might also be starting afresh after previously receiving bad feedback. Such sellers are marked with a circular arrow icon beside their name.

It's also always best to contact the seller and try and straighten things out if you've had a bad experience before you leave negative feedback. Sellers (and buyers) take umbrage at unexpected negative feedback and this is often how disputes and arguments start off.

Different Types Of Auctions

The proxy bidding auction process is what made eBay famous, and what makes it so addictive for buyers. But the various ways with which you can be tempted to part with your money are growing as eBay develops from an auction house into a broader trading platform. There are a handful of different styles of auction, and as many fixed-price sales systems, all with their relative pros and cons.

Reserve Price Auctions

The first variation is a **reserve price auction**. Like a traditional auction, this has a minimum price, preset by the seller, for which they are willing to sell. The twist is this reserve price is invisible to buyers. An item listing never shows what the reserve price is, only that it exists and has or hasn't been met. This is why you might sometimes be the first to place a £5 bid on a pair of shoes starting at £1, only to have your bid rejected. If you make a few more bidding attempts you'll realize that the item has a reserve price. But the proxy increments rule still applies, so if you make a bid of £10 and the reserve price turns out to have been £8, you are now the winning bidder. Unless anyone else comes along, the shoes will be yours for £8.

Dutch Auctions

Also known as Multiple Item Auctions, a **Dutch Auction** is a method of buying in bulk, but it's complicated, relatively unpopular (with only a few hundred running at any given time) and it's possible to end up being obliged to buy a lower quantity of items than you actually wanted in the first place.

Restricted-Access Auctions

These are for **adult-only goods**. To gain access you have to have a verified credit card on file with eBay (for ID checking, rather than billing) and to have agreed to the **Mature Audiences** category's terms of use, which is only available for US residents. Wonder why – unlike Google – searching eBay on innocuous words rarely if ever accidentally returns "adult-only" results? That's because anything porn or sex-related is listed as a **Restricted-Access Auction** and all such items are never included in searches, or the **What's New** and **Hot Picks** sections which pop up on the home page.

Second-Chance Offers

If the winner of an auction fails to pay, the seller is allowed to choose the next highest bidder and offer them the item instead, known as the **Second-Chance Offer**. Sellers also do this if they successfully auction an item but have duplicates available. Launched in 1991 (and previously known as Personal Offers) this is a particularly popular system for buyers on eBay Motors when bidders fail to meet the reserve price of a vehicle.

Different Types Of Fixed-Price Sale

Outside of the world of auctions, the aforementioned **Buy It Now** option is one of a set of fixed-price purchasing mechanisms, which was launched in the summer of 2002. It revolutionized the site, allowing businesses large and small to use it as a platform to sell – as opposed to auction – goods direct. A year later countless home businesses were using Buy It Now (aka BIN) as their backbone, to say nothing of the likes of Disney and IBM who also adopted the system. Here's a quick look at how BIN and various other fixed-price options work:

Buy It Now

It's very simple to buy using BIN. You read through the listing, click and pay (but remember that BIN prices are always exclusive of shipping). An auction seller can also include a BIN price giving you the choice of biding your time and bidding, or cutting to the chase and buying a product there and then. If that's your style you can use the **Search** panel on the left of the category listings to only show BIN items.

Get It Fast

Like a spin-off from Buy It Now, **Get It Fast** comes in the form of a logo alongside items whose sellers have stated that they will ship goods within one day of receiving payment. Beside the logo you'll see an approximate arrival time for the item, based on an estimated number of shipping days plus one day for handling.

Best Offer

If you want to get the best deal you can, and aren't afraid to haggle, then look for items listed with a **Best Offer** option. This is an optional extra on some (but not all) Buy It Now listings that allows a prospective buyer to contact the seller with an alternative, lower price. It's up to the seller to decide if they want to accept your "best offer" but if they do, note that it's not a suggestion, it's as binding as winning an auction, so you have to be prepared to show the colour of your money. At the same time, the seller is obliged to immediately close off the item, even if someone comes in with the full Buy It Now price straight afterwards.

Ad Format

Finally, there's the **Ad Format** system which first appeared in the Real Estate section. It's like a "classified ad" in that you don't actually buy anything at all.

Chapter 3

If you see a listing you're interested in you just click to submit your details; the seller then gets in contact with more information on the property or item in question. Ad Format sales have started to move into new areas and are now also an option in categories like **Websites** and **Businesses for Sale**, **Trade Show Booths**, **Prefabricated Buildings**, **Travel**, **Speciality Services** and **Everything Else**.

How To Pay

Despite what eBay might have you believe, there is actually a multitude of ways that you can pay for your items. Some are good, some are bad and some can be very ugly. The most popular by far is **PayPal**, a payment process that has been thoroughly embedded into the online auction experience since eBay acquired PayPal Inc. in 2002 (to the tune of $1.5 billion). It's very straightforward to use but not without its pitfalls or alternatives. We'll come on to PayPal with an FAQ (Frequently Asked Questions) section after considering the various other methods of payment you might be asked for by a seller.

Cash Or Cheque

If you're going to pay by traditional means – for example, by sending a cheque or money through the post – then you'll need the seller's contact information. You'll receive their email address when you win your item, which is your cue to make contact and find out their postal address. If you lose this info, just go back to the original item listing and click the **Ask Seller a Question** link. You may find that the seller gets in touch with you first, and most professional ones will. Either way, buyer and seller are obliged to make contact within three working days of an auction ending.

Your first thought might be to pay by **cash**. Many buyers do, but only for very, very low value items. The problems of paying by cash are obvious – no proof that payment has been made, and a high risk of your money getting lost or stolen en route. And if you ever come across a seller insisting they are paid only in cash, then be very suspicious – they are most likely fraudsters.

Sending a personal or cashier's **cheque** is another straightforward alternative. You'll have proof of payment and can stop the cheque being processed if you begin to experience problems with the seller. Whenever you send a cheque, include a covering letter with your name, address and the item numbers of the goods in question. It's surprising how many sellers report just

Wire Transfer Woes

On the subject of payment methods to avoid, so-called **instant cash wire transfers** have a poor reputation for online payments. If there's a situation where a seller has taken the money and run, more often than not they would have been insisting on an instant cash wire payment, like those offered by **Western Union** or **MoneyGram**. No buyer protection is offered and it's very difficult to track down the recipient of the funds should there be a problem. Again, if a seller is requesting payment *solely* via this method then be wary.

Of course **Western Union** is used all the time for legitimate reasons, most often for sending money to someone you *know*, for example a relative travelling abroad who has had their passport and wallet stolen. You send the money and they can walk into any outlet – wherever they are – and collect it, without having to show ID. This is obviously great when using the service with people you know, but useless if you're buying from a complete stranger.

Another popular scam that revolves around Western Union is by fraudulent sellers who suggest you wire money but to a fake name. They will suggest that only when you have received the goods and are happy with them should you change the recipient name so that they can collect their money. Do not even think about it. You can find out more about the company and read its fraud protection **FAQ** at: westernunion.ca/info/faqSecurity.asp.

receiving solitary cheques in the post. As user IDs rarely match people's real names they have little or no hope of figuring out who the money is from or what it's for. It's also a good idea to make sure that your address and the item number are on the cheque, just in case it gets separated from the covering letter. Remember that most sellers you're buying from are people, not businesses, and so aren't geared up for particularly efficient admin. The easier you make it for them to process your payment, the more likely you are to receive your goods on time.

Money Orders

Money orders are a dying method of payment, previously popular for international transactions. You might still want to consider them as an alternative to cheques. The pros and cons are exactly the same, although you'll have the additional hassle of buying the money orders in the first place. Just like cheques, money orders will delay the arrival of your goods, though, as sellers won't despatch anything until the money has cleared and gone into their account.

Chapter 3

Escrow

More than any other, **Escrow** is a payment method that's totally loaded in the buyer's favour. You pay your money to an Escrow service, at which point they tell the buyer to send you your item. When you've received it and decided you are happy you then inform Escrow and they release payment. Unlike most other payment methods that are free, Escrow will charge up to fifteen percent of the item price for their service. So it is only ever be recommended for high-value purchases. While you may be tempted anyway, few buyers will accept payment by Escrow because of the time lag between item despatch and money received – often up to eight weeks.

The big warning that should accompany any mention of Escrow is to always make sure you are paying into a legitimate service, because fraudulent sellers have been known to set up fake Escrow websites as a means of stealing money. Escrow.com is the one to use for UK and US residents and a list of approved Escrow services around the world can also be found there.

Credit Card

Credit card is probably the most secure and easiest form of payment for goods on eBay. There's just one problem: very few sellers – unless you're buying from eBay Stores or eBay Motors – can accept it. So while you can rest easy when you pay elsewhere online that your credit card company will protect both your identity and your liability, you'll be hard-pushed to find someone selling that bargain antique from their front room who is geared up to accept a credit card payment, which is where PayPal comes in…

PayPal

The downsides of all these existing payment methods led to the launch of PayPal in 1998. In 2002 the company was acquired by eBay itself and by 2005 it had 96 million users in 55 different countries, topping American Express. It may have some significant downsides – which we'll come on to – but for any-one who plans to make more than one purchase on eBay (more than 75 percent of all auctions are paid for via PayPal, after all) it's a very attractive proposition.

How exactly does PayPal work?

To start using PayPal on eBay you'll need to register at paypal.com to set up an account and then add funds either by transferring money from your bank

Sending Money With PayPal

Aside from being an eBay payment method, you can also use PayPal to "email money" to anyone with an email address, even if they don't have a PayPal account set up. Log into PayPal and enter the email address of the recipient, along with the amount and the currency you want it sent in. Click **Continue** and follow the prompts. The seller receives an email from PayPal saying you're sending money. As soon as they click to accept, the funds are transferred from your PayPal account into theirs. If they don't have one, they have the opportunity to set up a PayPal account there and then.

account or by providing your credit or debit card details. Of course, once you start selling on eBay and **receive payments via PayPal**, they too will contribute to your available balance.

As for paying on eBay via PayPal, it couldn't be simpler. Once you either buy an item outright, or win an auction, you will receive an email with a "Pay Now" link in it. Click this and log into PayPal to confirm your payment. Job done. Similar links will also appear on your My eBay page.

What does it cost?
It costs nothing to sign up to PayPal to pay for goods or to send money. It's the sellers that fund the system. Not only is it handy for eBay buys, there are also 42,000 other online businesses that accept PayPal, from Napster to Dell, all of which are listed on the PayPal website.

How can I get up and running?
It's a straightforward process that can be carried out either from paypal.com or paypal.co.uk. Choose a **Personal Account** if you only plan on buying. But if you think you might do some selling on eBay, then consider the **Premier** and **Business Accounts**. You then provide your personal details, choose a user name and so on. All your PayPal activity can now be managed from the control panel you see when you log in. It revolves around a set of self-explanatory tabs, labelled **Send Money**, **Add Funds** and so on. Don't forget to click the **History** tab, which provides the PayPal equivalent of bank statements. But remember that all of your PayPal activity takes place online – there's no paperwork.

Why do people rate it so highly?
Quite simply, convenience. Although PayPal is fiddly to get up and running – especially when you have to verify the bank account details you've lodged – it

makes paying very easy. You can go from winning an auction, or choosing a Buy It Now, to completing payment in only a half dozen mouse clicks. And that includes notifying the seller of your delivery details (which are held on file with PayPal), any special packing requirements and generating receipts for both parties.

Surely it can't be all smooth sailing?

Like most things, PayPal is fine until something goes wrong. When it does, they can be notoriously difficult to deal with. A lack of telephone contact and automated responses to emails are the most common gripes. On the one hand that's understandable – the company does have 25 million customers. On the other, it's unforgivable, given that they process billions of dollars' worth of transactions every year, taking a cut on every single one.

It would be wrong to think of PayPal as a normal bank or credit card company. For a start, it doesn't protect you in the same way that paying by credit cards does. You won't immediately qualify for a refund if your goods fail to turn up. Furthermore, the amount of disgruntled users who have logged in to find their accounts or transactions frozen – with no explanation – is significant. For more on the PayPal backlash check paypalwarning.com and paypalsucks.com.

Are there any alternatives?

Several, but none of them are owned by eBay, so they just don't have the visibility or integration with eBay that PayPal enjoys. The leader is **NoChex** (nochex. com). It's very popular with anti-PayPal sellers, who are themselves well worth looking out for as they'll often offer a discount on items if you pay by NoChex. The downside of NoChex is that it's only for UK residents. But other pretenders to the throne include **e-Gold** (e-gold.com), and **Neteller** (neteller.com).

The Golden Postage Rule

So you've paid for your bargain item. But how much did they say it would cost to ship? The golden rule is to **always check the shipping or postage costs** the seller is quoting. The BIN price or the bid price rarely if ever includes postage. And you always have to pay the shipping fee the seller has stated in advance – there's no haggling after the sale.

Just think of Chris Ollerenshaw, from Dukinfield in Manchester, who bought a bargain RAF bomber for a winning bid of £15,102.03 in November 2004. He didn't bank on the transportation costs from its Blackpool Airport home amounting to over £20,000, which meant he had to sell the plane back to its original owner!

Other postage pitfalls include the many unscrupulous sellers who demand inflated postage costs – alongside very low starting bids – in the hope that you won't notice, get carried away at the thought of a bargain, and be obliged to pay them much more than you had planned. Before you're happy with a shipping fee, check what it includes. Too many mobile phones are mailed in paper envelopes (even when the seller is charging the same as what another might ask for using a padded envelope). The result? Cracked or broken goods, with little means of comeback. No bargain is worth the price paid if the goods don't arrive in one piece.

Play By The Rules

eBay only works if people stick to the ground rules it is based on. The majority of these are common sense, but most new users have questions when they start bidding and buying. Other new users try and think of how to sidestep the rules, especially when they have a bargain in their sights. But there's really no point and, if you're reported for rule-breaking, eBay has a notorious policy of suspending or cancelling an account first and asking questions later. The rules for buyers can be found in detail at pages.ebay.com/help/policies/buyer-rules-overview.html. Give them a cursory read before you get started, or absorb these five main points:

1 You can't sidestep an auction Emailing the seller to make a separate offer is not permitted. Once the auction starts, that's it.

2 Bids are binding There's no scope for changing your mind. If you bid on something and win it, it's yours.

3 Reserve prices are secret If you bid high to find out what it is, you'll be obliged to pay that high amount should you win.

4 Bids can't be retracted for any reason other than accidentally entering the wrong amount If you win something you have to pay for it, and the shipping costs (whether you'd factored those in or not).

5 Shill bidding is prohibited Even though it's very easy for a seller (under another eBay identity) to place extra bids to artificially inflate an auction price, this is prohibited. There's very little eBay can do to stamp this out, except for relying on the good nature of the majority of its users.

But rule bending does take place. A classic example was during the public outcry against touts using eBay to auction tickets for the Live 8 charity concerts. Some users wrote letters of complaint asking for the auctions to stop, whilst "eBay vigilantes" simply bid £1 million on each ticket and then refused to pay, rendering the auction useless. It worked, but both parties lost out. The Live 8 touts were banned from eBay but the vigilante users also had their accounts suspended.

Disaster Recovery

What happens when goods don't arrive or **fakes and counterfeits** do? These are the problems of buying anything by mail or online, via auction or elsewhere, so you need to know your options.

Firstly, consider that there could be a misunderstanding. Perhaps the seller is trying to contact you and failing, or vice versa. The most common reason for this is if you have an overactive spam filter that's blocking their emails. Or maybe your email address has changed and you've forgotten to log your new one onto your eBay account.

If the seller really isn't playing ball then you'll need someone to mediate. There are two options, the first being eBay's long-winded but well-meaning "Item Not Received or Significantly Not as Described Process". This is a step-by-step process for buyers and sellers designed to track down both parties, and get them talking. Find it at pages.ebay.com/help/buy/item-not-received.html. Alternatively you can go off-site to a mediation company like **SquareTrade** (squaretrade.com) whose ODR (Online Dispute Resolution)

system provides a web-based forum and a panel of mediators who will hear both sides of the story and try and sort things out.

Another way that disputes arise is from leaving **bad feedback**. As mentioned earlier in this chapter, sellers don't take kindly to negative feedback and will often retort with even worse comments about you. Before you know it, you're in a "flame war" which can get out of hand. It's very hidden away on the site but, if you need it, eBay's **Mutual Feedback Withdrawal** policy is worth investigating. You can find it at pages.ebay.com/help/buy/disputes. html. Feedback wars are even more damaging for high-value buyers and sellers, which is why eBay Motors offers its own **Independent Feedback Review** area at pages.motors.ebay.com/services/independent-feedback-review.html.

What To Buy...

Collectibles

With seven million auctions about to close on any given day, this is the second largest eBay category and represents a massive portion of buying and selling thoughout the site. In fact the amount of goods deemed as "collectibles" has meant this category has completely outgrown itself, becoming unwieldy and messy. With more than four thousand sub-categories, all you can do is surf through rather than coherently explore this area. The most popular collectibles will soon become apparent, and a straw poll at time of writing shows the top five to be:

1 Postcards & paper (1,397,456 listings)

2 Comics (1,111,954 listings)

3 Decorative collectibles (519,206 listings)

4 Advertising (496,609 listings)

5 Animals (353,865 listings)

Picture Reality

You'll find many items are listed with a picture alongside but be aware that there's no saying for certain that the seller themselves took the picture. With books and music especially, sellers will often just use a picture found elsewhere on the Web to include in their listing.

Chapter 3

eBay has been compared to the world's largest flea market or car boot sale and the collectibles category is the reason why. After all, where else could you find a choice of 13,514 *Star Trek* trading cards, alongside 1243 pre-1970 metal lunchboxes, 14,197 buttons and 417 butter churns?! Go direct via: collectibles.ebay.com.

DVDs & Movies

The demise of video tape and the rise of **DVDs** has lead to a boom in buying movies via eBay: DVDs because they're lighter and cheaper to buy by mail, and video tapes because – as everyone switches formats – millions are being

Popular Goods
What is there the most of? The twenty busiest categories are:
1 Women's clothing (699,194 listings)
2 DVDs (335,997 listings)
3 Men's clothing (308,013 listings)
4 CDs (286,888 listings)
5 Women's accessories and handbags (221,485 listings)
6 Children's clothing and shoes (210,302 listings)
7 Pottery and china (204,376 listings)
8 Decorative collectibles (196,222 listings)
9 Postcards and paper collectibles (179,027 listings)
10 Records (171,936 listings)
11 Women's shoes (171,366 listings)
12 Girls' clothing and shoes (129,116 listings)
13 Necklaces (127,814 listings)
14 Dolls (127,399 listings)
15 US coins (124,213 listings)
16 Glassware (117,625 listings)
17 Advertising collectibles (116,957 listings)
18 Action figures (116,849 listings)
19 Militaria (111,426 listings)
20 Comics (109,567 listings)

Find What You Want Faster...

You can sort goods by time, price, payment type or distance from you. So if you're on a budget, sort by "Price: lowest first". Or if you want something urgently, select "Time: ending soonest". Some categories also include a **Product Finder panel**, which makes the needle in a haystack process of finding the product you want a little easier. The digital cameras finder lets you search only for those with a certain optical zoom type, or resolution.

thrown out, or rather thrown online, often selling for very low prices. You'll find two and a half million movies categorized by genre, rating/certificate and condition. What does this tell us about our viewing habits? Action/adventure, drama, comedy, and children's programmes, in that order, judging by the amount of material bought from this category. Go direct via: dvd.ebay.com.

Music

The music section has always been a great place to pick up cheap CDs and records. Add 1.5 million records to three million CDs and other sundry formats and you'll find a choice of five million releases here. But this section's reputation for money saving is fast changing as sellers get wise to postage and packing as a way of making profit. In the past you might get a bargain CD for £1 and pay a reasonable £1 postage and packing. Now you'll find most CD prices starting from £1.99 – no matter what they are – and postage costs sitting at a standard £2.50. Which starts to make impulse buys a thing of the past. Go direct via: music.ebay.com

Drill Deep

eBay is shy of promoting the fact that highlighted items (where the seller has paid a little extra in return for a prominent listing) always come first in search results or category listings. So if you search for watercolour pictures priced lower than £40, you'll see all of the highlighted auctions first and the cheapest might be £10. But it's only once you've scrolled through all of these that you'll see the rest of the auctions, which might include many pictures under £10. This is only a recent modification – in the past all sellers were mixed in together. But this new system, which means a more talented but meagre independent artist could be pushed fifty pages back in a search – has caused uproar in the artistic community that eBay had initially caused to thrive.

4

Selling On eBay

For Maximum Profit (And Minimum Effort)

There was a time, pre-eBay, when if you had something to sell you placed a classified in your local newspaper. You would have reached an audience of anything from a few thousand to a few hundred thousand potential buyers. If you had a lot of items to sell – from maybe a wardrobe or loft clear-out – then you would have had a garage sale, or headed off to the local car boot. But eBay changed all that.

It's just as easy to sell an item on eBay as it is through a classified ad (and much less hassle than a car boot or yard sale). And your customer base is somewhat larger: 181 million worldwide to be precise. That hideous painting you received as a gift and could never bear to hang on the wall? Chances are one of eBay's users would adore it. In fact, nowhere is the old adage truer than in the world of eBay sales: one man's trash is another's treasure.

eBay Apps

IzaBiza (izabiza.com) offers an audio version of eBay for US users. When you're out and about you just dial their (toll free) number, enter the item number followed by the # key. An automated attendant will then read back the number of bids, highest bid and time remaining. The best tool purely for sniping via your mobile phone is called **UnwiredBuyer** (unwiredbuyer.com). You transfer the list of auctions you are watching over to them and register your mobile phone number. Then, when there are minutes left on the auction, the system calls you – not a text message, but an automated attendant – to check if you want to bid up or stop bidding, the details of which you provide through your phone's keypad.

Making That First Sale

It's not a million miles away from filling in a form to place a classified ad. Once you've signed into eBay, click the **Sell** link and, from there, the **Sell Your Item** button. It's then a six-step process:

1 Choose how you want to sell The basic choice is between a fixed-price sale or an online auction. Or you can offer both options.

2 Select the category you want your item to appear in There is a countless choice of categories, but all are presented in a simple drop-down menu.

3 Write your listing's title and description Like any ad you might write, keep it clear, concise and factual.

4 Add images You can then add some pictures to your listing and choose some "promotional enhancements", such as bold text, a second category to appear in or special listing status. We'll come back to all of these add-ons and options in more depth later on in this chapter.

5 Price & postage The other details to add at this stage are financial. What's the auction's starting price, and reserve price? How would you like to be paid? And how much do you want for postage? Now is the time to enter these details before...

6 Review & submit Take a moment to review the whole listing before clicking the **Submit** button. Then you're done. Within a few hours the world will be able to see your auction and start bidding.

Chapter 4

How Much Does It Cost?

It costs nothing to start selling on eBay but the first time you go to use the **Sell Your Item** form you'll be asked for your credit card and bank details for security checks. When you list any item for sale you have to pay an insertion fee, whether your item gets bought or not. The insertion fees are pretty low, for example £0.20 for an item with a starting price of £1.00, up to £2.00 for an auction starting at £100. If the item doesn't sell you have nothing more to pay. But if it does, eBay will take up to ten percent of the final sale price in commission, what it calls a **Final Value Fee**.

There are a whole load of other ways you put money directly into eBay's coffers, and these revolve around **Upgrade and Picture Service fees**. For example, it costs extra to have an item subtitle or for your item title to appear in bold text. If you are feeling very flush, you can even pay for your listing to be featured on the home page.

There are costs associated with pictures too. While everyone gets to place one picture in their listing as part of the insertion fee, you pay extra for additional pictures and also for large – or **supersize** – images. You can find a full breakdown of eBay's charges at pages.ebay.com/help/sell/fees.html (pages.ebay.co.uk/help/sell/fees.html in the UK).

To find out how much you owe eBay for selling, it's easiest to log into **My eBay**. Click the **Account** tab, and from there, **Fees**. You'll see a full list of your auctions and sales, along with what types of fees are owed as a result. eBay will also despatch a monthly invoice to you, which you'll see flagged up under **My Messages**.

---

55 Careful Considerations

When you try to sell something on eBay, the headline or title you give your listing can be no longer than 55 characters. So you have to make each and every word count if you want to attract bidders. The golden rule is to write what buyers might be searching for, not what you want to say. So save thoughts of using terrible eBay clichés like "amazing" and "l@@k" to the actual listing, if at all. No one searches for anything "amazing", after all. Another tip is to turn the previous chapter's trick of finding bargains by searching for misspellings on its head. For example, if you're selling an iPod, you might want to refer to it as both an **iPod** and an **i-Pod** in the title if there's room, thus accessing a whole extra set of potential customers.

Payment is quite straightforward. You can either pay these monthly invoices by **PayPal** – of course – or by allowing eBay to **directly bill your bank account**, credit card or debit card. For the traditionalist there's a more convoluted printable coupon system, if you want to send off a cheque or money order.

What To Sell?

People first sell on eBay for one of two reasons. Either they've got something specific to offload, or they don't really know what they want to sell, they just want to try and make a bit of extra cash. If you're in the latter camp, then there are whole shelves of books out there advising you what you might want to sell on eBay, but all amount to nothing more than the kind of advice you'd get if you were considering what to sell at a car boot sale. The chance to make some money comes when you combine this common sense with knowledge of what sells particularly well.

Possibly the most detailed, useful and free guide to what you might sell is eBay's **What's Hot** list. Be prepared for a completely no-frills approach. No graphics, no pictures or colour, not even a webpage. Instead you'll find a forty-page PDF file tucked away at pages.ebay.com/sellercentral/hotitems.pdf that's updated every month. It goes through every category, listing them as either "Hot", "Very Hot", or "Super Hot" based on both growth in the number of bids and the number of items being listed. What's "Super Hot"? In **Baby** it's

---

Most Popular Purchases

1 CDs (there's one bought every eleven seconds)

2 Women's clothing (one piece every twenty seconds)

3 Men's clothing (one every thirty seconds)

4 Toy cars

5 Cell phones (one every minute)

6 Laptop computers (one every two minutes)

7 Handbags

8 Gold jewellery

9 Cars

10 Football shirts (one every five minutes)

nursery décor and diapering. In **Cameras** it's camcorders, and in **Cell Phones** it's accessories. You get the idea.

What Can (And Can't) You Sell?

It would be wrong to think you can "sell anything on eBay", and it's worth taking some time to find out what falls inside and outside the rules, especially because if you don't play by the rules your account could have its privileges altered or even be suspended. Click to **Help > Is My Item Allowed?** where you'll see a full list of the goods eBay terms as either "prohibited", "question-able" (OK to sell under certain conditions) or "potentially infringing" (in terms of copyrights, trademarks and so on).

eBay continues to experience great difficulty in setting out black-and-white rules on **what can and can't be sold**, mainly due to the sheer diversity of goods that people want to sell. This is why for every rule there's always an exception. Tobacco is illegal. But tobacco-related memorabilia and packaging is fine, and highly collectible actually. Spectacles are not allowed, but sunglasses of course are OK. If only Captain Kirk had checked the rules – in November 2005 the actor William Shatner announced plans to auction his recently passed kidney stone on eBay for charity, calling it the "ultimate piece of *Star Trek* memorabilia". The only problem was eBay's strict **rule forbidding the sale of body parts**, no matter how famous their donor.

Clean Your Drives

Obviously you need to make sure that anything you auction is cleaned up and as presentable as possible. But one thing you might forget to clean – that could have disastrous consequences – is a **hard disk drive**, should you decide to sell yours on when upgrading a PC. Simson Garfinkel from Harvard University's Center for Research on Computation and Society claims to have bought almost 250 hard drives off eBay in the last few years, and to have found over three hundred credit card numbers on them. And in the summer of 2005 German company O&O Software conducted a similar survey, buying two hundred hard drives and finding more than seventy percent still stored sensitive personal and/or business info. What's more, Garfunkel says that a cursory surf of eBay's **Computing** category shows hard drives selling for much more than their market value – a sign that there are buyers out there specifically looking for "crocks of (data) gold". This is a warning for businesses too, with **Techweb.com** reporting a hard drive sold on eBay by a medical centre that contained 11,609 unique credit card numbers.

One area that the site won't be going near for a long time is pets. In December of 2005, it proposed a new plan to launch a classified ad service for pets but was inundated with users who could see it was open for massive exploitation. It would seem that if and when pets do appear on eBay in the future – if at all – it will be through a partnership between the site and pet adoption agencies.

Setting The Right Price

You know what to sell, but how much to sell it for and what kind of money can you expect to make? The easiest way to answer that question is to log in and click **Advanced Search**. Look for similar items to yours but make sure you've ticked the box to search **Completed Items**. This will give you access to the last three months' worth of completed eBay auctions, showing you whether items sold or not, how many people bid and what prices were reached.

This process is the essence behind **Terapeak**, an eBay market research company. For a monthly fee you can trawl previous auction details, and receive guidance on which category to place your items into. Trouble is, even for Terapeak's $16.95 per month you can still only study the last three months' of auctions. Music sellers though have a useful – and free option – in the form of **Popsike.com**.

The team behind Popsike.com are recording, trainspotter-like, details of every music sale made on eBay (and other online auction sites) and entering them into a database of their own. It's very rough and ready – they don't edit out duplicate listings or overtly cheesy sales banter – but it does provide you with a very accurate idea of what you might be able to expect to raise from

Chapter 4

Fine-Tuning

Here's a ten-point checklist to make sure your auctions and sales run as smoothly as possible.

1 Rotate gallery images To keep catching people's eyes, it's possible to change the gallery image in your listing more than once during the auction.

2 Amend any mistakes You are allowed to alter an item description while an auction is live as long as no bids have been received and the auction is more than twelve hours away from ending.

3 End an auction You can end the auction early, for example if the item becomes lost or broken, but not if there are fewer than twelve hours to go.

4 Cancel a bid If a bidder contacts you to back out of the auction, or if you have been unable to confirm the identity of a bidder, you can cancel some or all of the bids on your auction. But be careful – cancelled bids cannot be reinstated.

5 Manage your buyers If you are getting a lot of bidders and buyers and want to filter them, it's possible to set up a list of buyers that are blocked from your auctions. You might block buyers from a country you can't ship to, those that can't pay with PayPal or those that have low feedback.

6 Blocked Buyer Settings In February 2006 eBay launched the Buyer Requirements Activity Log. It sounds boring but it's very useful – showing you details of who and how many people your "block buyers" setting actually turned away, allowing you to fine-tune them for future auctions.

7 Approved Buyer Settings You can also set up a list of pre-approved buyers. These can bid immediately, leaving others to gain email authorization. But note that these run for any auctions you set up, not just those you specify.

8 Lower the reserve price If you fear you're in the reserve price trap then, as of September 2005, it's possible to lower the reserve price while an auction is still live although, you guessed it, not during the final twelve hours.

9 Make the most of feedback As soon as you have completed a transaction successfully, leave positive feedback. Also feel free to politely nudge buyers if they forget to leave you feedback.

10 Answer buyers' questions A real turn-off for those considering your goods is not having their enquiries responded to. And where it seems appropriate, always post your responses to the listing (you'll see the check box for this when replying to buyers' questions), as it is both useful to other potential buyers and shows that you are a helpful seller.

the auction of those embarrassing old Rod Stewart singles tucked away in your loft.

These guides and suggestions will give you a good idea of what you might make from a sale, and they'll also **help you set a reserve or Buy It Now price** if you decide to go down that route. But if you're running an auction the general rule of thumb is to **set your starting bid low**, certainly way under the level you might hope to finally sell at. Put yourself in your buyer's shoes: what's more attractive and exciting, being the first to bid on a pair of Nike Air Jordan XXs that are starting at £2.00, or finding an auction of a similar pair with a starting bid of £20.00? You would of course bid right away on the cheaper pair, and while it might take a few bids to get up to £20.00, by then lots of interested parties will have placed bids and a few bidding wars will have started which can do nothing but drive the price higher.

This is why so many auctions on eBay have a starting bid of £0.99 or $0.99, no matter what they're for. There's always a risk though that the bidding war scenario doesn't erupt – you make a loss and a lucky bidder makes a steal. But for many it works. "A piece of designer fabric we listed for a client usually sold on eBay in the $200 range", says eBay trader *goinginceamc*. "One other seller listed his designer fabric for $199 and received exactly that. We

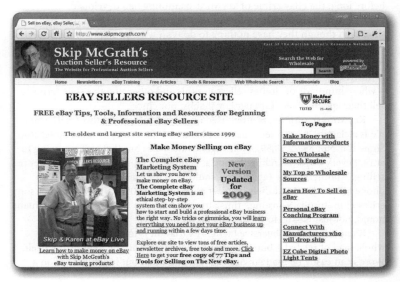

started ours at $9.99, generating furious bidding. Ours sold for over $400! This seems counter-intuitive, but we've found this occurs time and again…"

"I was having lunch one day with four of the largest PowerSellers on eBay, all were Titanium PowerSellers. Between them they sold over $35 million a year on eBay", says Skip McGrath, editor of the longest running newsletter for professional eBay sellers at skipmcgrath.com. Putting the whole starting bids idea into stark focus he "asked one seller, what was the best way to list an item on eBay? He replied, 'I list everything at 99-cents, no-reserve.' One of the other sellers agreed with him partially and the other two disagreed vehemently – kicking off a heated discussion that went on through dessert. One person's *secret* is seen by others as just another opinion…"

Tricks And Rule Breakers

The first classic trick for eBay sellers was to fill their item titles with supposedly **eye-catching phrases** like "LOOK!" or the more cringe-worthy "L@@K!" (or even unrelated, highly popular Web searches like "Britney Spears"). And while this still gets done by sellers hoping that people will *browse*, most people have realized that eBay items are more often found by *searching*. And not many people search for "L@@K!" So the rules got bent a little bit further and, before long, the eBay crime of keyword spamming had developed.

The process is simple – you add popular search words into your item title, even though they have nothing to do with what you are selling. For example, a title might be posted that read "Clear Glass Flower Bud Vase… Just Like CAMBRO" to attract people looking for Cambro vases, even though it wasn't one. It's a variation on the slightly less unlawful "shabby chic" line – where hundreds of clothes sellers use this and other popular style terms to sell their apparel even if it's neither shabby, nor chic.

Keyword spamming is often used on **eBay Motors** and this (real) example is a classic: "Chevrolet: Chevrolet Nomad 1956 Chevy Nomad Street Rod Show Car Not 55,57,58,59,60." It's against the rules but that seller is going to attract every buyer searching for a classic-era Chevy, not just the year they're selling. Another classic (again, you couldn't make these up) is the mobile phone seller who listed their handset as "NOKIA 8800 UNLOCKED not sony ericsson motorolla Samsung," thus attracting anyone who searched on a main brand, not just Nokia, to their spurious listing.

It's not the only subversive tactic. A variation is to invisibly include a whole load of related – but not relevant – keywords in the item listing itself. Words can easily be made invisible by setting them out in white text, on a white background. It happens a lot with music auctions. Someone might have a Duran Duran CD to sell and in such invisible text on their listing they include dozens of band names – Wham, Spandau Ballet, and so on – from the same

era. eBay's search mechanism is none the wiser. The end result for the buyer? Simply that those searching for one of the unrelated artists lands on the auction and – the seller hopes - are tempted enough to bid or buy.

Then there are the real curve-ball seller techniques. Like those who sell **bootleg and pirate DVDs** and movies. They know that eBay will remove the listing if they include the word "bootleg", but not necessarily if they change it to "b@@tleg". Then there are the ones that list inexpensive goods for a sale price of £1 million. They know they'll never sell them, but they also know that some buyers will have their search results set to list by most expensive first. And if those that do see something they like, they might click on that £1 million item just to see what else the seller has available at a more genuine price.

Before you take inspiration from these sellers, note that **keyword spamming is against the rules** and – if spotted by eBay (admittedly highly unlikely given the amount of listings they have to audit) – your auction will be taken straight down. Besides, according to research by **Sellathon.com**, it doesn't actually work. Their **ViewTracker** software measures the amount of time buyers spend reading an item listing. They found that the average is 26 seconds. That sounds low, but they also found that if the item title turns out to be misleading or a mismatch, then the time plummets down to 2.9 seconds.

"Anybody who expects to make more money or get more bids by adding 'Britney Spears' or 'Paris Hilton' to their auction description is just deluding themselves", Sellathon.com's Wayne Yaeger explained to eBay guru Ina Steiner at **Auctionbytes.com**. "It doesn't work. It might make their hit counter go up, but that's all."

Chapter 4

Using Drop-Off Centres

Drop-offs were touched upon in Chapter 2's FAQs (see p.17). But what exactly are the pros and cons?

The Pros...

For a start they do all the hard work for you, from listing to payment processing and international shipping. They might get a slightly better price or quicker sale based on their site knowledge and high feedback rating as well. (The UK's **Auctioning4u** claims an average sale-through rate of over ninety percent, compared to forty to fifty percent for most eBay sellers.)

They can attract more potential buyers, as they accept many different payment types and might have a professional photographic studio for item listings. It's also secure – in that you don't need to disclose any personal information online, as you're selling through an agent. And most centres have high trust ratings based on their **PowerSeller status**. Most drop-off centres also act as **free mediators** should the buyer and seller of the goods disagree on anything from authenticity to condition. They are also a good means of **protection from fraud** – the buyer gets the upper hand as most centres will not pass on money earned to sellers until the buyer is happy with the goods.

...And The Cons

Most centres take a thirty percent commission on every item they sell for you. Many also have a **price threshold** and won't consider selling anything valued at less than say $50. They might also come with **extra charges**: not only is there the commission to consider but many centres will charge you extra for taking photos for the listing, and ask you to cover their eBay and PayPal fees. All centres know that starting an auction at $0.99 is a good way to get attention, but some have been known to impose a $19.99 surcharge if the customer wants their goods to start at a higher price.

Drop-off centres also have a reputation for charging buyers **extortionate postage fees**. And even charging $5 to cover packaging if the buyer collects in person. And while centres may have experience of writing great listings, you may have a far better knowledge of your particular item and its market. Finally, there aren't any regulations for drop-off centres, unlike auction houses or pawnbrokers, their closest relatives.

Trading Assistant Checklist

Choosing an eBay drop-off centre is easy – you know where they are because they have a fixed store front. But it's more difficult with a **Trading Assistant** (TA) because most operate purely online. So make sure you've ticked off the following seven points before you give them your items to sell.

1 Don't look for, or accept, promises as to what your item will sell for Even the most experienced TA can't predict what the market will pay on a particular auction on a particular day.

2 Get a firm, written timeline of what the TA proposes to do Find out when they plan to start and end the auction, their no sale policy, their buyer return policy, etc.

3 Make sure you've completely checked them out Check their feedback, ID and contact details. Check with other people who have used them. Check their sales activity and the prices they've raised. Check everything. Then double-check it!

4 Ask how much experience they have of selling your particular item If they plan to do their research after they've received your item, how much will that delay the auction going live?

5 Get a signed receipt All TAs should provide a signed receipt when they take delivery of your goods ready to try and sell them.

6 Provide as much information as you can about your items Give any backup documentation, history, details of previous owners and the like. Anything that will help the TA make a compelling listing and maximize return.

7 Make sure you meet your TA Most suggest a quick meet-and-greet to find out what they're like, and a second to hand over your goods.

If you've covered the points above then trust the seller. Most prefer to be left to do business as best they know how, and rarely have the time (or inclination) to answer questions about why they've chosen a particular title, category or starting price.

The bottom line? It's a close call but for many sellers the pros outweigh the cons. So if you have an attic to clear or a business to liquidate, or if you plan to use eBay as a one-off for a high-value item, then go to a drop-off centre. But for everyone else, forget it. Having digested this book you'll have as much, if not more, eBay knowledge than most people running drop-off centres so make the sales yourself. Otherwise you'll just be giving your money away…

Creating Compelling Listings

Can you deliver a good sales patter? The answer has to be yes, if you want your item to fetch a high price. The Web equivalent of a compelling sales spiel is a **compelling item listing**. This one, scrollable webpage is your chance to make the item you're selling as attractive as possible. First you have to cover the basics. Make sure your listing is as descriptive as possible and that you've detailed:

1 The exact condition Even if it's brand new, include any minor flaws or scratches.

2 Full size/dimensions

3 Brand/manufacturer This should include the make and model, including any relevant part numbers.

4 The year the item was made Or a best guess if you don't know. Even a decade (1940s, 1950s, etc) is better than nothing, as many buyers search using such terms.

5 Notes on colours And even textures for antiques, with reference to supporting pictures.

6 Original cost One other thing you should include is a note on what the item cost you originally, or what it currently retails for in the shops. That combined with a low starting bid will have browsers' fingers twitching on their mice.

Make sure you tackle all these points as clearly as possible. Use a list or set of bullet points to make the listing as straightforward to understand as possible – it will get read in many different countries after all. And it's amazing how many item listings contain dozens of lines of continuous babble, with not a full stop or comma in sight. On the subject of language, consider some of the many **acronyms** buyers and traders will understand. Is your vinyl record **NM** (near-mint), or is your DVD player **FS** (factory sealed)? Getting up to speed with these terms will definitely help you but then again don't overuse.

Your Title Counts

Before you get too involved in writing up your listing, make sure your **title is as compelling as possible**. Doug Feiring has been running a blog of seller tips at auctioninsights.com since 1999 and says the best titles use "keywords

that potential bidders use to search listings ... solves a problem ... make a reader curious to know more ... is simple and easy to read and understand (and) exhibits professionalism."

Tweaks & Widgets

There are lots of tweaks and widgets you can use to make your listing look as alluring as possible. eBay's **Listing Designer** options (found in the **Seller Central** area) has over two hundred colourful layouts into which you can place your text and pictures.

Hidden Value?

It's not always possible to give your TA detailed background info on the item you want them to sell, despite the recommendation in the Trading Assistant Checklist (see p.49). As eBay TA *going1nceamc* reports, "We once had a deck of cards we listed for a client. All the client knew was the deck was about a hundred years old and the face cards featured Swedish royalty of that time. There was nothing to be found about these "Boman" playing cards. This deck was in fantastic condition and the client was one whose items generally did quite nicely on eBay, so we took a chance and started the bidding at $19.99. After these sold for over $2500, it occurred to us that sometimes items are so rare that info is scarce..."

Chapter 4

With a basic knowledge of HTML, the language used to design webpages, you could make your listing look just as colourful and even more impressive. eBay's own HTML guidelines (under **Selling > Listing Your Item**) are badly worded and confusing. If you want to do the coding yourself you're far better off trying the HTML Basics section of a site like **WebMonkey** (webmonkey. wired.com). But for those who want to concentrate on selling rather than programming, the Web is awash with pre-designed sales pages, or templates. Trouble is, most are garish, gaudy and border on the plain ugly. There is no end of **eBay templates** out there – a simple Google search will prove that. It's more a case of finding one that looks half respectable and less like an accident in a 1970s wallpaper factory.

When you have a page you're happy with, you need to think about how to promote it and a **gallery listing** is well worth considering. The gallery fee is only $0.35 but for that your picture appears beside your title in search results, and also in a special section of results when buyers do a Picture Gallery search. It affects your bottom line too. Research has found that gallery listings are ten percent more likely to sell, and gain a final price that's twelve percent higher than their unillustrated competitors.

There are even more compelling statistics on listings that have **bold**

Audio Listings

Don't just make your listings easy to read, make them easy to hear by using podcast services like **Podcastalley.com** to record and host audio descriptions of your items. Or take things further with **SellersVoice** (sellersvoice.com), a monthly subscription service that takes away the hassle of recording and editing your audio messages. You just call a toll-free phone number and record your sales pitch, which is then embedded in your eBay listing as a flash audio file, which means that most people can play and hear them, no matter what system they use.

titles. This costs an extra $1.00 but has been found to generate a 24 percent increase in bidding, and increase the final sale price of an item by 21 percent. There's also a way to make your sale show up sooner in a list of search results. Though they'd be loathe to admit it, all eBay auctions are put in two pots, first and second class. The first-class ones – otherwise known as **Featured Plus!** auctions – show up first when you do a search. Scroll through them all and then you'll come to a horizontal line, and below it you'll find the standard, or second-class auctions.

Pictures

Not only does a picture paint a thousand words, but all eBay research shows that you are far more likely sell your item if it's accompanied by a photo. In fact the better the pictures, the more likely you are to make a sale and – if it's an online auction you're running – the higher the final price is likely to be.

With most households today owning a digital camera (or at least a mobile phone with a reasonable set of photo functions) it's easy to illustrate your listing. First the basics: **give a good selection** of images. Not a complete photo album, but six images are more likely to sell an item on eBay than just providing one.

As to what size and resolution you should use, there's no need to go crazy. The standard resolution of images online is 72dpi, and you don't really need to upload images larger than about 700 dots across (or 400–600kb in size). You can go bigger, but remember that buyers with slower Internet connections might struggle to view the full-sized version of the image that eBay offers.

If you are providing six images, you have a good chance to show your item from a set of different angles. And try some close-ups and long shots too. Whether it's clothes or furniture, a buyer needs to be able to effectively see all round the item as they size it up. In terms of the actual content, keep it plain and simple. So if you can lay out your items on a plain background (like a sheet, or up against a white wall) then do so. It sounds simple, but viewing pictures off a computer screen is never easy – you should do whatever you can to make your items as appealing to the eye as possible.

Tip: Web-Based Tools

If your camera doesn't spit out the exact size image that you are after, use an online tool such as the one found at pixlr.com to resize or crop your images for free.

Chapter 4

Camera Tips

Two main tips when choosing a digital camera to use for eBay product shots. Firstly, don't worry about paying for hi-resolution. One megapixel is detailed enough for a picture that will only ever be seen on a computer screen. Secondly, make sure it has a macro setting, to allow you to focus in on some close-ups.

Photo Spam

Don't be tempted by the photography equivalent of "keyword spamming" (see p.46). Adding a picture of a bikini-clad girl to your auction listing of power tools might increase the number of people viewing your listing, but not your sale price.

Car Pics

Robert Soar from **Solent Overlord**, a military vehicle club (solentoverlord. co.uk) has sold several cars on eBay and says that "a minimum set of pictures should include exterior views from each corner of the vehicle, interior shot(s) and engine bay."

If it is clothes you're selling, you'll find that other eBay sellers – your competition – are increasingly using **mannequins** to model their wares. They're far more effective than laying stuff out on the floor, or having your mum do the modelling for you, and can be picked up cheaply in the **Business > Office & Industrial > Retail & Shop Fitting** category. Buyers like to see second-hand goods in the best condition possible, so as well as stating what packaging you have to offer in your listing, show it in your pictures. If it came in a box, has a particular tag or special bag then make sure these show up in at least one of your photographs.

There are no shortage of software packages to manage and upload your pictures but it's worth considering eBay's own **Picture Manager** system, if only for the fact that you know all pictures will be compatible with your listings. And you won't have any problems transferring the pictures to eBay as they'll be hosted by the site itself. It's essentially a repository for all of your auction-related pictures, where you can sort them, rename them, assign them to different sales and store them for safekeeping after a sale, should you ever need them again. Find it at pages.ebay.com/ picture_manager.

It's not free of course, and prices for using Picture Manager start from $9.99 for 50MB of storage. So you might alternatively want to consider hosting the pictures on your own personal website. It shouldn't cost you much, if anything, as most ISP services provide a certain amount of space for free. You transfer your pictures to your personal space and then link them into your listings using HTML. FTP is the software you'll need to perform the transfer and you can find a choice of systems at download.com.

A Question Of Timing

There is a right time of the day, week and even year to sell online. First of all, don't worry about when your auction should start. As most people place bids or **snipe** in the closing hours then you need to think carefully about when your auction will *end*. **Sundays, Mondays, weekends in general and evenings are all high-traffic times**. So don't just click to start your auction right away when you're in the final **Review & Submit** phase of the **Sell Your Item** form; work five days back from those traffic times and set your auction to start then.

There's also a right time of the year to sell. eBay makes public which categories it plans to promote on its home pages in the coming months. You can see the calendar for yourself at pages.ebay.com/sell/resources.html. So if you have something to sell that fits into a category that will be highlighted soon, resist the urge to try and sell it now and hold off until that promotion comes round. You could benefit from thousands of extra browsers.

Gaining Inspiration From The PowerSellers

A June 2005 tally by AC Neilson International Research found 724,000 people sell on eBay not to offload unwanted Christmas gifts but to generate a regular income. These so-called **PowerSellers** often do so by setting up an **eBay Store or Shop**, using some of the professional tools and software available, sourcing their stock from wholesalers or, increasingly, drop-shipping and acting as an intermediary between the world of international business and the browsers and buyers they originally started out as.

eBay knows that in order to keep going it needs to encourage as many people to sell on their system as possible. And it needs the sellers that it has to sell as much as they can. The more people sell, the more money eBay

Chapter 4

makes and the more it grows. So, just like the McDonalds-style stars it awards users based on their feedback rating, the highest possible accolade is to become a **PowerSeller**.

It's an exclusive club that you can't apply to join. You just have to ramp up your sales and wait for the call, or rather email, from the powers that be. eBay loves hierarchy, even among PowerSellers, of which there are five levels. To make it as a **Bronze PowerSeller** you'll need an overall feedback rating of 100 of which 98 percent is positive and – most importantly – be bringing in a minimum of $1000 sales per month (£750 in the UK). The levels rise up through **Silver**, **Gold**, and **Platinum** up to **Titanium PowerSellers** who shift a staggering $150,000 (UK £95,000) of sales each month. They have to maintain that success too, for three months straight, otherwise they drop down to the next level.

The main benefit of becoming a PowerSeller is the kudos and trust it inspires among buyers and browsers by having the little logo beside your ID. Such a small icon can make people want to shop with you far more readily than anyone else. eBay also pushes the boat out in terms of support for these users. Bronze PowerSellers receive **priority email support**, Silver and above get **free phone support** and Gold and above get a **dedicated member of staff at eBay**.

Once they've achieved this god-like status, PowerSellers also get access to two restricted areas of eBay. One is quite unremarkable, the **PowerSellers discussion forum**. The other – **Reseller Marketplace** – is rather more mouth-watering. Launched in June 2005, it's a category where manufacturers, liquidators and wholesalers sell off stock in bulk lots, often at very low prices.

The forum is a closed shop, available only to PowerSellers. Worth a look – and free to everyone who wants to pick up a bit of PowerSeller insight – is the **eBay Sellers Unite blog** at powersellersblog.com.

eBay Stores

Setting up an **eBay Store** (stores.ebay.com), or **Shop** (shops.ebay.com) as they're known in the UK, is like setting up your own website within eBay. The main attraction is that you get your own distinct URL that's searchable from outside of the site, and able to appear in results on Google and other search engines. Store URLs like **Best4Baby**'s stores.ebay.co.uk/best-4-baby and alternative energy consultancy **Network 6000**'s stores.ebay.com/network-6000 are much more memorable than your average eBay trader's member profile page, which for user **oolichan** who sells camera parts in Seattle for example, is feedback.ebay.com/ws/eBayISAPI.dll?ViewFeedback&userid=oolichan&iid=7608386359&frm=284!

Setting up an eBay Store allows you to show all of your items in one central list, whether they're **Buy It Nows** or **standard auctions**. You also get access to a third sale format called **Store Inventory**. These are fixed-price sales that stay online longer than a Buy It Now. eBay charges a lower fee, too, but they will only ever appear in your store listing.

There's a **subscription charge** of $15.95 per month which – depending on how much you want your store to be promoted throughout eBay – can be scaled right up to $300 per month. On eBay UK, prices start from £6.00 per month but the charges are very hidden away. In fact they're not even in the eBay Shops part of the site – they're in the Help section: see **Help > Selling > Listing Your Item > Fees > Shop Fees**. Whatever you pay, the **Seller Manager software** is thrown in along with some handy traffic reporting systems which show what routes buyers are taking as they click around your Store.

The design of your Store is completely up to you. As with auctions, you can use a predetermined template or invest in some HTML expertise to make your storefront look professional. The header, the left-hand menu and so on are all customizable and your Store also includes its own search box, which is very handy if you have a large inventory. You can also add your own categories, so your products are presented exactly how you'd like.

Chapter 4

Good 'Til Cancelled

To save relisting popular items in your Store you can tag them as **Good 'Til Cancelled**. This will make them automatically relist every thirty days until they sell out or you cancel it yourself.

Selling via a Store will increase your bottom line. Research has shown that sales increase by 25 percent in the first three months after opening a Store, although the most recent data is from 2002. But that increase won't come automatically. Just as in the High Street, the success of any Store is down to the amount of promotion you put into it. With eBay Stores you can add **special promotional boxes** on the page itself and, to drag customers in, you can edit the meta-tags (the search words that help it show up prominently in Google) and design and distribute **online flyers and mail-shots**.

Know Your Market

The first step to becoming a PowerSeller, and the basis of any professional activity on eBay is **market research**. As English eBay raconteur Oliver Goehler once told *The Daily Telegraph*, "Concentrate on something you have knowledge of, because you need to know your market in order to get good prices." Goehler (olivergoehler.co.uk) is one those people newspapers love to write about; he asks the question: "why would I work a nine to five day for a fraction of the money I'm making now? With eBay, I can make a big chunk of cash without having to make a big amount of effort". So if you want a piece of this action, there really is no match for experience, trial and error, and your own research.

The best way to get instant market research is, as the previous chapter describes, to work through **eBay's completed listings**. Surfing those will show you what people are buying, which categories are busy and what kind of prices you can expect to sell for. There is no shortage of websites and self-appointed gurus ready with their guides to "what's hot" on eBay but the majority just take their lead from the site's own category-specific research, which you can see for yourself by going to **Sell > Seller Central > Category Tips**. One of the more plain-speaking and informative third-party market research companies, however, is the aforementioned **Terapeak** at terapeak.com.

In 2005 eBay started publishing some very useful research on what buyers are doing when they enter eBay, which pages they go to first, how often they come and how long they spend there. One of the aforementioned pages. ebay.com/sellercentral/buyers.pdf's most useful yardsticks shows the ever-fluctuating popularity of the different categories. **Collectibles** has always been streets ahead of the others, with **eBay Motors** and the **Computers** category in an ongoing battle for second place. Third place is equally hard fought, between **Clothing**, **Toys** and **Electronics**.

But this is by the by. Very few successful sellers coldly choose a niche and begin trading. The majority work in an area they understand and have experience of, either from their professional or home life, or from colleagues or friends, and develop existing experience rather than start afresh. And the clever ones take a niche they know and **find a new angle**, which itself can only come from research.

Inspiration!

Who are the biggest sellers on eBay? Auction management software company **Novato** has been ranking the top five hundred eBay members based on feedback rankings since 2002 and you can track their results at nortica.com/userarea. The top five jostles around each month but boils down to the same five users:

1 Everyday Source which sells cheap PDAs and gadgets from the Far East. Feedback score: 350,701, Store: stores.ebay.com/everydaysource, ID: *everydaysource*.

2 Eforcity selling mobile phones and MP3 players. Feedback score: 315,783, Store: stores.ebay.com/eforcity, ID: *eforcity.*

3 Accstation selling cell phone accessories and DVDs. Feedback score: 309,914, Store: stores.ebay.com/accstation, ID: *accstation.*

4 iTrimming who sell much the same thing, but with printer cartridges too. Feedback score: 295,381, Store: stores.ebay.com/itrimming, ID: *itrimming.*

5 Jay and Marie who sell bargain CDs as spotlighted elsewhere in this chapter. Feedback score: 278,977, Store: stores.ebay.com/jayandmarie, ID: *jayandmarie.*

5

Amazon Marketplace

The First Real Alternative To eBay

I n the late 1990s and early 2000s, if you wanted to sell your stuff online, make a bit of extra cash and find some bargains, there was only one place to go – eBay. Yahoo! and all manner of other Internet giants tried and failed to set up competitive sites and eBay remained number one. But then along came Amazon. It had been there from the start of course, selling books, then music and films, and then all sorts of household goods. And then Amazon set up Marketplace, a system to allow you and I to sell our goods alongside their own stock. Have you ever searched for a book on Amazon, seen it priced at, say, £9.99, and then spotted a line underneath stating "four new and used copies, available from £4.99"? That's Amazon Marketplace in action.

It's certainly on a par with eBay and, in many ways, has the edge. Writing up a compelling eBay sales listing can be a time-consuming job. Whereas with Amazon, you don't write up or design a listing – you just **find the prod-**

uct you want** from their catalogue, **add some notes on condition** and shipping and **click Submit**. All of which takes about one minute.

But there's the rub. You can list almost anything for sale on eBay (and boy do we mean anything!). But with Amazon it has to already be in their catalogue. The other key difference with the mighty eBay is that with Amazon Marketplace, **you set the price you want to sell at**: they don't do auctions.

As a result, a strange, downward-spiralling price war often takes place over an item. On eBay, the bidding starts with a low price and the buyers take it higher and higher. On Amazon, a seller will start off with a high price (or, at least, just a shade under the standard retail price that Amazon itself is selling for). Other sellers will spot this and undercut you, then you realize and undercut them and, consequently, **prices can tumble** before your very eyes, sometimes in a matter of hours. Great news for buyers of course, but it can be pretty disconcerting for sellers.

How much do Amazon get?

"The main disadvantage of selling on Amazon is the commission fee", says Sophia, a UK-based Amazon Marketplace user who trades under the ID of *bambamsophz* and also sells on **Play.com**, **eBay** and **CEX** (cex.co.uk). "Last week for example, I made £167 and ended up with only £125 to myself.

61

Chapter 5

Which means around £42 was taken in commission." *Bambamsophz* also has some good advice on what sells well on Amazon. "I sell textbooks mainly on Amazon", she reports, "and find that it is the best site to sell books on … For fiction books and a few others it varies, but the place that I go to if I want a textbook is Amazon, so it stands to reason to sell on there." (You can read more of her advice on Microsoft's **Ciao** reviews website at ciao.co.uk/Amazon_co_uk__Review_5748930).

What sells well?

So what else sells particularly well on Amazon, from a home trader's point of view? The way to find out is to read through the site's own charts. Click either the **Amazon Bestsellers**, or **Amazon Daily Blog** links from the main home page and you'll get an idea of what sells well. **Books**, **CDs**, **software**, **cameras** and **electronics** are all worth selling on Amazon. But if you have a wardrobe full of DVDs and videos, you might be as well trying your luck with them on an eBay auction, as the prices most sell for on Amazon are pitifully low. The current US Marketplace price for the Special Edition DVD set of *Charlie's Angels*? Just $0.91. And the current UK Marketplace price for a VHS of *Four Weddings and a Funeral*? More than 100 copies are available from a sorry £0.01.

Reversal Of Fortune

Christmas 2008 was Amazon's busiest ever, despite the recession. In the last three months of the year it saw sales climb eighteen percent to $6.7 billion, and this was due in no small way to the Marketplace traders. eBay, on the other hand, had a disappointing end to 2008. Its revenue in the same period dropped – and for the first time ever in the company's history.

Book Care

As books are the main seller on Amazon, you need to make sure the ones you are selling are in the best possible condition. The step-by-step guide at **AbeBooks** (abebooks.co.uk/docs/RareBooks/bookCare.shtml) covers everything from mildew to rips, tears and sticky marks. There is also a good collection of book care links on many US public library websites, for example **Tipecanoe County Public Library**'s bibliophile section at tcpl.lib.in.us/find-a-good-book/book-care-and-repair.

Of the products that do sell well on Amazon, **computer software** is one. And the trick here is that if you're going to sell on your old games and applications, don't hang about. As soon as a new version is out, you might well see yours drop in value. "For instance, several months ago I could sell the original *Sims* video game for around $12.00", says Amazon trader *MyProductAid*, in his Marketplace selling guide on **HubPages** (hubpages.com/hub/How-to-Sell-on-Amazon-Marketplace--Part-1). "However, since the release of *The Sims 2* and greater versions, the original game is being sold for roughly $4.00 on Amazon Marketplace. In some cases the game can be purchased for as little as $2.00."

How does the Amazon payment system work?

One key difference between selling on Amazon and eBay – or anywhere else for that matter – is how payments are processed. There's no need to send cash or cheques, or deal with PayPal. Amazon effectively sits in the middle and processes all payments, keeping the buyer's and seller's account details private. They also guarantee each transaction – so you don't have to worry about the PayPal chargeback scenario (see p.15) outlined in an earlier chapter. When a buyer selects your product they pay Amazon there and then (saving weeks on the eBay process already). You then immediately see the funds appear in your Amazon seller account, and those funds are transferred from Amazon to your normal bank account every two weeks. And unlike other online sales sites, you don't pay a charge when you transfer your profits.

Chapter 5

Amazon: Step-By-Step

Take that book you want to offload in one hand, your mouse in the other, and try this step-by-step guide to selling it on Amazon. It will take you all of two minutes and may yield a healthy profit.

1 First, sign up You'll need your bank account details to hand and, in the UK at least, an invoice address. This is also the moment to decide on the name of your store or trader ID, as each seller can set an ID that's different to their Amazon login name.

2 Find your title You now log the book you want to sell. The quickest way to do so is by typing in the ISBN number, EAN (barcode number), UPC (US barcode number), or ASIN (Amazon's own unique product ID). Or you can just search by typing a rough approximation of the title into the search box.

3 Check the edition You'll then see a set of choices – the various versions, editions, formats and so on that match what you typed. Click the item title to read more about it – and check it's the same as yours – or to see how much it's selling for, both new and used. Or click **Sell Yours Here** to get your copy listed.

4 State the condition and add any extra comments.

5 Set your price This is the fun part – you see how many other people are listing the exact same item and at what price. It's time to decide what price you want for yours. Do you wait for something you deem reasonable? Or do you undercut the current lowest price in the hope of a quick sell?

6 Set shipping options Choose where you want to ship to and that's it. Your item will now be live, and will appear along with any similar editions in the **New And Used** section when someone browses for that particular book. Once the goods are received by the seller they can leave **eBay-style feedback** about you, and you can reciprocate.

List And Relist

Listings stay on Amazon for sixty days. On day sixty you'll receive an email reminding you to relist it. Unless you're in urgent need of cash, it pays to keep relisting everything you have that doesn't sell, as you never know when your buyer will come looking.

Mailing Your Items

One thing Amazon is very hot on is **despatch times**. All Marketplace sellers agree to despatch their items **within two days**. It's not enforced – or checked up on – but buyers are quick to complain if they don't receive their goods within a few days of buying. Of course you can't mail goods out promptly if you're away from home so, if you're going on holiday, Amazon allows you to temporarily remove all of your listings. You can find out how to do this at amazon.co.uk/holiday-settings.

Pro Merchants

If you have a great deal of goods that you want to sell, then you might consider becoming a **Pro Merchant**. Pro Merchants pay reduced fees on every item they sell, but there is a **monthly subscription charge**. It's very much aimed with businesses in mind but if you sell more than thirty products each month it could well save you money – or rather help you earn more money. The easiest way to find more info is to click the Pro Merchant links you'll find on the **Sell Your Stuff** page at amazon.co.uk/gp/seller/sell-your-stuff.html.

Amazon Vs eBay

With both sites claiming upwards of eighty million users – so coming neck and neck on prospective customers – how exactly does Amazon differ from eBay? Here are some of the main ways, from a home seller's perspective.

Sales Talk

On eBay you can design a whole page about the item you have for sale, complete with pictures, animations, even **video and audio**. On Amazon, you only get a thousand characters with which to make your comments – book-sized proportions for **Twitter** users, but sellers often leave this space blank. That's a mistake, as there's a lot you could say that might swing a buyer towards you rather than one of the possibly hundreds of others listing the same item. Are your items always despatched next day? Or might you include a bonus CD or book with each one? Is it still gift-wrapped or sealed? This is the place to state your case and try and win the sale.

Chapter 5

Postage

On eBay you set your own postage amounts (which is where some naïve sellers have lost money, and other unscrupulous ones have milked extra profit). On Amazon, buyers are automatically charged an extra delivery fee when they order and these fees differ depending on product and destination. Amazon then passes the delivery fee (minus an admin charge) on to the seller.

Grading

Once again, on eBay this is an open playing field while on Amazon it's strictly controlled. On eBay you can grade your item however you like – these are no common guidelines and of course this is open to massive misrepresentation and misinterpretation. On Amazon, on the other hand, you can only grade your item in one of nine ways. And if the buyer disagrees they're sure to say so in the feedback they leave, which means that sellers rarely misrepresent their goods.

Feedback

eBay wins out here as the feedback system – which they pioneered – has a real sense of community spirit. Meanwhile, Amazon breaks down and gives a much more accurate sense of your reliability as a seller, though fewer buyers bother to leave any feedback. They get an automatic reminder to do so, but only two weeks after they made their purchase.

One curious aside: the stigma of low feedback does less harm to sellers on Amazon. "You will see sellers with a much lower feedback percentage still be successful (on Amazon)", says Jason Watson of **AuctionArena.com**. "There are several sellers with a percentage as low as 92 percent who sell thousands

---

Amazon's Options

Amazon has a dizzying array of tools for sellers, and it's easy to get confused and click your way down the wrong track. Put simply, **Amazon Advantage** and **Fulfilment by Amazon** (aka FBA) are both professional distribution and listings services for distributors and business ... so of little or no use to you if you're reading this book. The services that are worth checking out are **Amazon Associates** and **Amazon Marketplace**, the latter headed up as simply "Sell Your Stuff" from the **Amazon Services** section on their main home page.

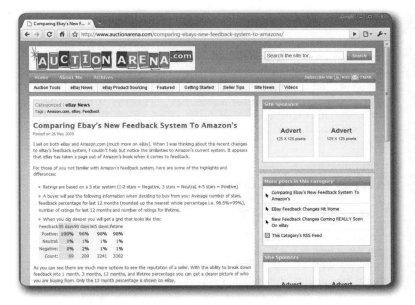

of items a year. There are hundreds of successful sellers with a 96 percent rating." You can read his detailed analysis of the two warring sites' worlds of feedback at auctionarena.com/comparing-ebays-new-feedback-system-to-amazons.

Price Limits

From a seller point of view, you'll never chance upon a rare book or item to sell and become a millionaire on Amazon. Unlike eBay where the sky's the

---

Bookmark It

Clicking through Amazon to get to your seller account is surprisingly tricky. There are just so many links from the home page. So take this link and bookmark it: https://sellercentral.amazon.co.uk/gp/homepage.html (and note the "https") and you'll get straight to the "front door" every time. If you are in the US, use https://sellercentral.amazon.com/gp/homepage.html.

limit in terms of bids, the maximum you can sell anything for on Amazon is £2000.

As both sites have their pros and cons, the savviest sellers work both to their advantage. Like **GetRichSlowly.org** user Greg C, who runs a business selling books online. "Amazon doesn't charge listing fees and you can list and relist an item for however long it takes", he says. "Depending on the competition, sometimes it's easier to set and get the right price on Amazon." The downside? "Other times everything is selling for a penny… It depends. There are so many different variables. I have actually 'flipped' books from Amazon to eBay before…"

Amazon Associates: Earning Money From Clicks

If you run a website or blog, there's another way you can use Amazon to make some money and that's by signing up as an **Amazon Associate**. The process is simple: you run adverts on your site and if someone clicks through and buys the product in question, you get a referral fee. With over 900,000 members, it has to be the most popular referral marketing system in the world, and it certainly boosts Amazon's sales, with estimates running at up to forty percent of its revenue coming from the ads its Associates host for it.

To find out more, head to affiliate-program.amazon.co.uk in the UK, or affiliate-program.amazon.com in the US. Compare the two and you'll find one sore point among its users: the US proclaims you can "earn up to fifteen percent in referrals by advertizing Amazon products." But in the UK it's only ten percent.

Either way it's a win-win situation – you **earn money from referral fees**, and Amazon wins more sales. But there's no point just putting up some random ads for products you like the look of on your site or blog. Try these top tips to get your referral fees as high as possible.

1 Match products with your content It sounds obvious but pays dividends. If you're blogging about a particular type of food, make sure you have relevant recipe books linked right alongside.

2 Give your visitors some choice If you don't want to link to specific items, you can embed an Amazon search box on your site – it will still yield the same commission if people click through and buy something.

3 Check performance Make sure you check to see which links and products are generating the most amount of click-throughs on a regular basis. These are the ones you need to make sure remain highlighted.

4 Cross-sell If you're blogging about food, then you don't just have to link to cookery books. How about linking to cookery tools and gadgets, or books about the area your food in question comes from?

5 Keep track of discounts There are always sales going on somewhere on Amazon so, if you have a generalist blog or website, you're as well to link to the products that are currently on special offer, to try and get the most amount of people attracted and clicking through.

6 Keep it timely In high faluting marketing talk, it's called "trigger-marketing". But in plain English, it's a case of linking to gifts and products you think your Dad might like in the run-up to Father's Day, and so on.

7 Keep an eye on the Amazon Associates blog It's at affiliate-blog.amazon .co.uk (affiliate-blog.amazon.com in the US) and is where they update you on what's selling, what's discounted, and also special competitions where – for example – Depeche Mode webmasters were once offered free tickets and merchandise for placing the highest number of click-throughs from their fan pages.

Chapter 5

There are downsides, of course. "Payments are made every three months", according to Ash Pearson, who is in the informed position of being both an Amazon Affiliate and hardened eBayer. "Most other affiliate programs and publisher sites will offer monthly payments. [...] The Commission earned is not very high, so you may have to make a lot of sales to get any decent type of payment." You can find more of his balanced account of Amazon from an eBayer's perspective at reviews.ebay.co.uk/Amazon-Affiliate-Program-Amazon-Associates_W0QQugidZ10000000008191520.

Pay Per Post is one of a stream of websites that give you a token fee every time you write a blog post or product review for them – another chance to earn money from your web activity. Others worth considering are Pay Per Post's social networking spin-off site **SocialSpark** (socialspark.com), **PayU2Blog** (payu2blog.com), **ReviewMe** (reviewme.com), and **SponsoredReviews** (sponsoredreviews.com).

All of which fits perfectly with the frugality ideal – choose a product, find the best price, and then save a little more by getting paid to write a review of it!

6

Bargain Hunting On Amazon

Wish Lists And More...

Having devoted a whole section of this book to bargain hunting on eBay, you might wonder why we're only tackling how to bargain hunt on Amazon with this little chapter. The answer is simple – Amazon is a catalogue-based website with fixed product titles. If you search for something, chances are you'll find it. Or you can browse the discount sections – amazon.com/gp/movers-and-shakers for example. eBay, on the other hand, is like an every-man-for-themselves scramble to buy and sell, and finding your way in the noise is sometimes pretty tricky. While Amazon is like a trip to a quiet catalogue showroom, eBay is more like a trip to a Moroccan bazaar.

Chapter 6

Amazon Helpers

Most Amazon users will know the **Wish List** feature, which allows you to bookmark products you might like to purchase at a later date and, if you want to, share that list with friends and family. But there are also a couple of great apps available that take this one stage further. These let you set a target price for each item you're after and, when the app spots a listing that matches or falls below your desired price, it will send you a message – via email or SMS – so that you can then step in and buy. Check **Wish Radar** at wishradar .com and **WishlistBuddy** at wishlistbuddy.com to find out more.

One of the most inspirational websites for finding bargains on Amazon – and elsewhere on the web – comes from Yan Bezugliy, who describes himself as "a Java Swing programmer from 9am to 6pm and an entrepreneur and web developer at any other time." He runs **ProBargainHunter.com**, a blog about online shopping. He has created various handy tools such as **Deals Cloud** (dealscloud.com) which animates the current bargains on the **FatWallet** (fatwallet.com/forums) and **SlickDeals** (forums.slickdeals.net) forums.

"Like many men I hate shopping", Yan says. "But strangely enough I enjoy shopping online … The difference: the one is a chore; the other is a *sport*."

Cheap And Free Postage

Another aspect of Amazon which might save you money is called **Prime**. You pay a flat monthly fee and, in return, they waive all shipping charges on the goods you buy. But which products are Prime-eligible? Use IT consultant and blogger N Kishore's home-made search page to find out at nkishore.com/amazonprime. The way to avoid paying for postage altogether is to buy goods totalling more than $25. But what about that annoying moment when you realize your order total comes to just under, say $24? Before you decide to grin and bear it and pay shipping fees, pull up a "Filler Finder" website, which will search Amazon for $1 goods – or anything of the low value you enter – so you can add it to your order and avoid those sometimes hefty charges. **Amazon Filler Item Finder** (filleritem.com) is by far the easiest to use but **PriceTaker** (pricetaker.com) and **SlickFillers** (slickdeals.net/slickfillers) are also worth a look.

Search Tips

Yan's most popular post to date covers a system of customizing your own Amazon search URLs to find discounted goods. You can read it in detail at probargainhunter.com/2006/11/28/amazon-shopping-tips-and-hacks or use a simple search table – that covers both UK and US – at probargainhunter .com/2007/01/16/amazon-discount-shopping/#discount_table.

While a similar search-based version of this idea is available at **Jungle Search** (jungle-search.com), Yan's pages are simpler, and friendlier to read. But as he says himself of the discount info these systems provide, "Take the results you see with a grain of salt … I noticed that Amazon often stocks items for a very long time. As fast as the prices for electronics go down, it is

---

Amazon Auctions?

Amazon tried and failed to enter the online auction space in the early 2000s, which is why everything we buy and sell on there now is at a fixed price. When it started Amazon Auctions in March 1999, most people expected it to overtake eBay and for a while it looked good. It bought the company **LiveBid** to allow live streaming auctions and also hooked in major retailers such as **CameraWorld .com** while eBay was still concentrating on home sellers. But in the ever-jostling auction world, a furore over the sale of illegal weapons and porn, and changes in customer support, started a mass exodus of sellers. One of them went on record, telling **News.com** how "Lack of customer support is extremely apparent … I think (Amazon) missed the boat when Yahoo! dropped off the face of the Earth with their auctions…"

---

funny to see a 32" LCD TV listed for $15,000 and discounted down to $1000. That makes one hell of a bargain!"

For a simpler approach to seeing bargains as they appear, try the directory-based **Jangle** (jangle.net), **Spendfish** (spendfish.com) and their "Catch of the Day" newsletter. Another good place to swing by is the **Enjoy Deals** blog at enjoydeals.blogspot.com, which also highlights the biggest and best new discounts at **Buy.com**, **Dell.com**, **EndLess.com**, **Meritline.com** and **Staples.com**.

Part 3:
Other Ways
To Sell

7

The Alternatives

Why Look Beyond eBay And Amazon?

Do we really need an alternative to eBay and Amazon for selling our goods? The answer is always going to be yes, as sellers and consumers continue to use the Internet to find the best deals, be it discount goods, or the fairest set of fees, expenses and deductions for sellers. All of this translates into wildly varying fortunes for the online giants. "eBay blames its shrinking revenues on the melting economy", reported Cade Metz in *The Register* (theregister.co.uk) in spring 2009. "But sales continue to expand over at Amazon.com". Why is this? *Register* readers were quick to respond with a catalogue of complaints against eBay – or "feebay" – which boiled down to increasing commissions, decreasing margins and an annoyance at paying a cut to both PayPal and eBay (as one owns the other) every time an item gets sold.

So, what are our other options? There are a handful of full-on competitors, and an ocean of wannabes, clones and cash-ins. Almost all of them have something worth recommending, or testing out, so are put under the microscope here.

Shopping.yahoo.com

First up, Yahoo!'s **shopping.yahoo.com**, worth checking out for its **Near Me** button which links in with Yahoo! Maps (maps.yahoo.com) giving street maps and driving directions for items you might collect rather than buy mail order.

While Yahoo!, eBay and Amazon battle it out in the US, there have been defeats on all sides elsewhere. In 2002 Yahoo! threw in the auction towel in Europe, pulling out of the UK, Ireland, France, Italy, Spain and Germany, shutting down its websites and – in a deal struck with its rival – actually pointing users back to eBay as its "preferred online auction site".

They'd not had an easy ride, it has to be said. Yahoo! spent several years at the centre of a firestorm in France over the sale of Nazi memorabilia. It started in 2000 when the **Union of Jewish Students** sued the site for selling items that were banned for sale in France. Then in 2003 the **Association of Auschwitz Deportees** attempted – but failed – to have the head of the site itself prosecuted on counts of "justifying a crime against humanity" and "exhibiting a uniform, insignia or emblem of a person guilty of crimes against humanity".

There may have been a paltry nineteen live auctions left on Yahoo!'s UK site when the doors closed, but hundreds of thousands of users around Europe were left stranded. Clearly the handshake with eBay wasn't too firm. If it had been, users would have been able to move their registrations and – most importantly in the world of online trade – their feedback status from one site to the other.

eBid

In the UK, however, there was one site that was willing to take on the customer base, feedback ratings and all, from Yahoo! – the nagging younger brother to these two elder statesmen, **eBid** (ebid.tv). Running a shade under 2.5 million auctions at any given time, eBid has all the same features as eBay. Feedback is called the same thing, even the "Meet the Seller" box is called "Meet the Seller", but they do have some interesting twists. It never charges a listing fee and, if you purchase a "gold" membership, you never have to pay a

final value fee. Music and clothes are the most popular areas of this site. But in music it's surprisingly not CDs that people are selling – it's **vinyl**.

uBid

Chicago-based **uBid** (ubid.com) is another significant auction site player and was founded in 1997. Rather than have high opening bids, or reserve price auctions, they encourage all items to start at $1 in an attempt to let the market decide the price of just about everything. This is a site to check for gadgets and PC hardware as almost half their sales come from their electronics and computing categories.

uBid has also always been a very secure place to go shopping. As the tech business magazine **ePrairie.com** comments, "Just as Apple's technology far outweighed IBM's and Sony's Beta was a superior approach to the VHS standard, uBid's secure platform has outlasted the rigours of fraud that have caused countless users to abandon eBay."

And More...

Outside of these big names, there is a hoard of young pretenders, hoping to get enough scraps – or disgruntled users – from Amazon and eBay's table to make a living. Of the many little-known but well-liked systems, these five are well worth a look:

1 iBootSale (ibootsale.co.uk) Calls itself "the UK's Online Car Boot Sale" and offers your first 25 sales completely free.

2 Google Base (google.co.uk/base & google.com/base) In development since 2005, Base allows users to make their classified ads and For Sale listings searchable via the World Wide Web and Google's own Google Product Search (products.google.com) for free.

3 Overstock (overstock.com) Long-running Amazon rival which promises "brand names at clearance prices".

4 Proxibid (proxibid.com) For its live audio and video webcasts of auctions.

5 Vintage Computer and Gaming Marketplace (marketplace.vintage-computer.com) For all your retro motherboards...

And there's more… Check out the link ebay-alternatives.co.uk, a site run by Lancashire PowerSeller and manager of **eempire.co.uk**, Dave, which lists at least 20 further bit-part players in the world of online sales and auctions.

Safety In Numbers?

All the other auction sites have some interesting features for sellers, and a new set of products for buyers, but none of them can match the sheer scale of eBay or Amazon. But perhaps if they joined together into some sort of consortium they'd have a chance? Unfortunately that's been tried, and it failed. In 1999 the **FairMarket Auction Network** was set up, combining the resources – and items – of a hundred different sites. It had some top name buy-in, too, like **Microsoft**, **Lycos** and **Dell**. And early signs were very good for the cartel: as soon as it was announced, eBay's share price dropped by ten percent.

But, try as they might, the FairMarket cartel just couldn't tempt users over. By the end of 1999 all one hundred sites combined only had a choice of seventy thousand items for sale. That year, eBay's listings had reached two and a half million. A year later the figures spoke for themselves – revenue of $3 million versus eBay's $97.4 million – and the end was in sight for what was a noble idea.

Chapter 7

Mash-Ups

A mash-up in the programming world is when you fuse one website's technology with another to create something new, useful and fun. Like this mash-up of **eBay Motors** and **Google Maps**. It allows you to browse for the make and model of car you want, then set how far you would be prepared to go and collect it. The site then zooms into a map of the US which is cross-referenced with eBay Motors to show you what's available and where. It started off as a page on its programmer's blog at trachtenberg.com/emgm but now resides at the far more appropriate URL of dudewheresmyusedcar.com.

Microsoft

Microsoft has tried and failed to become a serious player in online sales for DIY traders. First there was auctions.msn.com in the US, but the content was provided by someone else: **uBid**. Then in the UK (at msn.co.uk/ebayauctions) they partnered with **eBay**. Windows Live Expo offered a Craigslist/classified ads-type approach in the mid-2000s, with **MSN Messenger** alongside other chat and networking options. They're now pinning their hopes on a new search engine, Bing (bing.com), and its **Bing Shopping** offshoot. But it remains to be seen whether the venture will be a success…

Cooqy

If you still want the familiarity of buttons and categories, but agree that eBay's interface is hard work, then **Cooqy** (cooqy.com) might be the answer. It aims to display auctions faster by filtering out extraneous detail. It also adds some extra features of its own. There's an integrated map, you can view galleries of up to 48 items side by side, all "time remaining" details are animated, and all item photos come with a built-in magnifier.

"Shopping on eBay leaves a lot to be desired", the system's founder, Robert Yaeger, complains. "Cooqy's Web 2.0 technology overcomes the headaches…" You can even **colour code** it to suit your mood. "The ability to select an eye-pleasing colour theme can enhance the shopping experience", he adds, "by reducing eye-strain from eBay's high-contrast white background."

Webuyanycar.com

Selling your car can be fraught, and not exactly profitable. You could go for a **part exchange** and get less than you hoped for it. Or you could go for a

private sell and have to put up with tire-kickers, time-wasters and loose arrangements when it comes to banking the cash and handing over the keys. But the **UK Car Group** has an interesting alternative. Their website (webuyanycar.com) offers instant valuations and money for your motor. You handle the whole thing online and then drive the car to one of their 32 locations (normally housed within standard garages) around the UK. The website is a new venture but the UK Car Group has been in business for more than fifty years and, if you want to talk to someone real, they have a UK call centre running seven days a week. You can get your head around the whole thing with some useful video guides online (webuyanycar.com/sell-used-car-guide-videos/Video-guides.aspx) which cover every step of the process.

8

Half.com

Bargains On Classics, And Long-Term Selling

The longest-running website for selling off your unwanted books – which tops eBay and Amazon Marketplace in many ways – is Half.com. It's well known for both its fair and frugal sales and commissions and also for its doggedly loyal user base.

Half.com first hit the headlines when it launched in 1999, at the height of the **dotcom boom**. As hype and marketing took new companies off into the world of ridiculous publicity stunts, this site stole the show, buying its way on to the world map by getting the small town of **Halfway**, Oregon, to change its name to **Half.com**.

The company survived the **dotcom crash** and, by the time **eBay** came along and bought it up in 2000, it had 250,000 regular users. eBay's plan, of course, was to absorb the site into theirs, giving users two ways of selling and putting themselves head to head with the increasingly competitive **Amazon**. But they failed, twice, as Half.com users refused to switch over to eBay.

Those users had a strong voice, and they had a point. "It takes about 20 keystrokes to list a book on Half.com. It takes 20 minutes to list a book on eBay," blogged Half.com user *avocats* in September 2004, after eBay announced the sites would remain separate. "I'm a big eBay user but not for books and CDs. Half.com just makes sense, and there was no way I was going to convert.

Chapter 8

I'd just switch my book selling (and used book buying) to Amazon…"

Even incorporating some of the aspects of the site into eBay didn't work, and the users spoke up again. Head of the revolt this time was **Pia Calabretta**, a small trader of second-hand romantic fiction. "They've taken some of the aspects of Half.com and moved it into eBay," she told Silicon Valley's *Metro Active*. "When they bought (Half.com), they said, 'We are going to close Half .com, and we want you to join the eBay community. You will find the same ease in putting your books here.' It's not true. They haven't got a clue what a

Shipping Tips

Like its sister and competitor sites, there's a whole culture of **tips and tricks** to help you get the most from your sales on Half.com. California blogger Joshua McGee shares his knowledge at mcgees.org/2008/02/19/ebay-tips while Greg Inman in South Carolina has a whole stack of Half.com experience you can learn from at associatedcontent.com/user/369929/greg_inman.html.

The Long View

It often happens that you go to list a book, CD or game for sale on Half.com or Amazon Marketplace only to find other people already selling the exact same thing for 1p or 1c. But **GetRichSlowly.org** user Dave Farquhar (who blogs at dfarq.homeip.net) has some great suggestions on how to take the long-term view to try and still make a sale, rather than giving up at the first hurdle. "If you have something that's only selling for a penny on Amazon, check and see if only one or two copies are selling for that", he says. "If so, it's a temporary price war. Price yours higher and wait for the cheapies to sell. If there are dozens of them for a penny, either list it on Half.com [where the minimum price is 75 cents] and hope for the best, or don't bother…"

---

book is. You can see it in their website. They do not know what books are; there's more to selling a book than saying 'Here's the ISBN.'"

Half.com's users are so loyal because the site was designed very much with the small bookseller in mind. And, unlike an auction system or Amazon Marketplace (where listings expire after sixty days), if you log a book for sale it stays online until it is sold. No listing fee, and no hassle of relisting. Just a fifteen percent commission to Half.com when the item sells. In eBay's favour though – and in the spirit of the feedback system they pioneered – they listened to the users and, for now, both sites are set to coexist, no matter how uncomfortably.

Using Half.com

Compared to all of the other sites for selling, Half.com is very, very simple to navigate, because it only has six product categories: books, textbooks, music, movies, games and game systems.

If you're looking for choice, then eBay and Amazon Marketplace are your best bets. But if you are looking for serious discounts on current and recent releases, then Half.com is a great system though it's only priced in dollars and has **no UK equivalent or subsite** (unlike eBay and most of the other main sites in this section).

Although the site may be part of eBay, it's a **fixed-price**, Amazon Marketplace-style system. So you can see the standard, list price of a CD or book and – alongside it – all of the copies offered for sale by individual traders with their individual prices. It's also strikingly similar to Marketplace from a seller's point of view: you list products by **ISBN** or **UPC**, set your price and condition, and you're done, with payments handled by the site for you and your earnings coming every two weeks. Though one useful difference in their favour is an easy-to-use multiple item listing page at sell.half.ebay.com/ws/web/HalfMultiSellDescribe.

Another neat difference at Half.com is that the site will do a quick calculation on what percentage saving off the list price the lowest seller will get you, which leads to some very mouth-watering deals on classic every-home-should-have-one books and CDs, like these:

1 ABBA: Gold, Greatest Hits (CD): $0.99 (Save 92%)

2 The Beatles: Sgt. Pepper's Lonely Hearts Club Band (CD): $2.12 (Save 88%)

3 Madonna: The Immaculate Collection (CD): $0.75 (Save 96%)

4 Pink Floyd: Dark Side of the Moon (CD): $2.49 (Save 86%)

5 U2: The Joshua Tree (CD): $0.75 (Save 94%)

6 William Golding: Lord of the Flies (paperback): $0.75 (Save 92%)

7 Khaled Hosseini: The Kite Runner (paperback): $0.75 (Save 95%)

8 Harper Lee: To Kill a Mockingbird (paperback): $0.75 (Save 90%)

9 George Orwell: 1984 (paperback): $0.75 (Save 92%)

10 JD Salinger: The Catcher in the Rye (paperback): $0.75 (Save 89%)

So Half.com can certainly kit out your book and CD collection with ten all-time classics for less than $10 but, with prices so low, **can you use it to actually make any money?** "I highly recommend Half.com for anyone interested in selling or buying used CDs, books, videos or video games", says **Ciao** user *madsmon22*. "When I first discovered the site, I went through my house

---

Pricing Tip

So how do you price the items you sell? "Pay some attention to 'natural price points'", says GetRichSlowly.org user and **Amazon Marketplace** user *Poor Yorick*. "These are prices that people have been conditioned through years of retail to pay. People are comfortable paying $11.99 for something because, chances are, they've bought hundreds of items at that same price over the course of their lifetime. $11.73 is a bit stranger to them!"

Brooklyn Rules!

Selling on Half.com gives you a great idea of what's popular and where. "Seriously, what's up Brooklyn?" asks Atlanta blogger Todd Dominey (whatdoiknow.org) who culled his entire CD collection with an online sale in the run-up to Christmas 2006. "Whenever I had a CD that was kinda obscure, but really good, it *always* seemed to go to an apartment in Brooklyn. Good taste up there. Anything world, international, or sorta new-agey always seemed to land in California. Must be the sun..." You can read his full story – and a useful selection of tips from a seller's perspective – at whatdoiknow.org/archives/002960.shtml.

and gathered up all the CDs that we never listen to, videos we're tired of and books I was tired of looking at sitting on my shelf. I registered with Half.com and listed all my 'goodies' for sale. In four months, I have sold about $150 worth of the 'junk' laying around my house. When garage sale season starts back up, I plan on picking up CDs that I think I can re-sale on the site. I've only done this once so far, but I sold one I got for 50 cents for $7! Not a bad return on my investment!" Another user reports even larger profits. "During a two-year period, I netted $510.19 from selling books and CDs that were sitting around, collecting dust", reports *Mountain Girl*, a user on **Associated Content** (associatedcontent.com).

9

Craigslist, Gumtree & Rent.com

Classified Ads Sites With Millions Of Readers

If all the fiddly bits of listing and pricing puts you off selling your stuff on Amazon and eBay, and if you just want to place your second-hand goods in front of a worldwide audience, there are two humongous, free-to-use classified ad sites you can try. Craigslist and Gumtree both have their merits and idiosyncrasies, and both are examined in this chapter. But if you're planning on renting out your spare room to make some extra money, don't bother advertising it on these sites. Head straight to the third main Web property covered in this chapter – a spin-off from eBay, Rent.com caters well for both tenants and landlords.

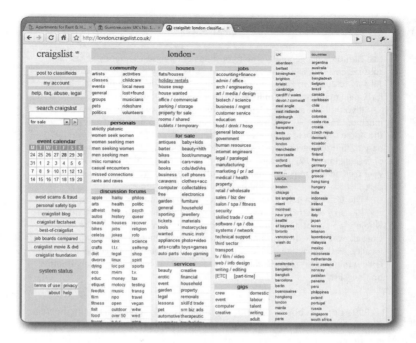

Craigslist

The parallels between Craigslist (craigslist.org) and eBay are striking. Both started in the mid-1990s as one-man Internet hobbies designed to hook people up and help them out. Craig Newmark was a consultant and webmaster who had arrived in San Francisco in 1993 and fell in love with the place, so he set up a forum to chat about his favourite hangouts, like the Anon Salon (anonsalon.com) venue and Joe's Digital Diner (telecircus.com/yeold/Digdiner).

Craig's Weirdest

Just a handful of the left-field, bizarre and oddball free ads that appear on Craigslist every day. As nominated by users, at craigslist.org/about/best.

- **20 May 09** Mow our lawn for a date!
- **15 May 09** Magic wand to solve life's problems.
- **13 May 09** Supersize Your Car.
- **13 May 09** Free roller coaster.
- **12 May 09** Seeking hot vet to figure out what the f*** is wrong with my cat.

Chapter 9

Craigslist

Like Gumtree, it's generally free to post ads on Craigslist and they've set up subsites covering all major US cities and some territories further afield, from Tel Aviv to Zurich to Egypt. 570 cities around the world, to be precise, although forty million of their fifty million monthly users are in the US.

If you think Gumtree is light on graphics and fancy layout, you won't think much of Craigslist – its appearance has hardly evolved in the last ten years, with the home page focused purely on functionality over form. The upside is that it's easy to find the section you're after. The downside is it has all the excitement of logging into a 1970s mainframe computer. But the real thrill is in placing your free ad and making some money off the back of it. Head to their FAQ at craigslist.org/about/help/faq to help get yourself started.

There's also a handy set of hints on avoiding scammers at craigslist.org/about/scams and their number one suggestion underpins the basic tenet of the whole site: it's not about global, it's about local. So, yes, there may be Craigslist sites all over the world but only buy and deal with the one devoted to *your* locality. As they say themselves, "Deal locally with folks you can meet in person. Follow this one simple rule and you will avoid 99 percent of the scam attempts on Craigslist."

1999's dotcom boom coincided with San Francisco's apartment shortage and Craig's new feature that allowed people to upload ads themselves, placing them directly on the site. As a result it grew in parallel to eBay and by 2004 was being used by more than ten million people every month placing **eight million classified ads** for jobs, houses and apartments and personals.

That year eBay bought a 25 percent stake in Craigslist. It had hitherto operated as a non-profit, advertisement-free entity, and has since remained surprisingly true to those ideals. "They have no interest in asking us to change that in any way", Craig's CEO **Jim Buckmaster** explained at the time. "They're happy with us having our full autonomy."

In fact rather than changing Craigslist, eBay took inspiration from it and launched its own classified ads website in March 2005. Craig had only ever really concentrated on the US after all and with **Kijiji** (kijiji.com) – meaning village in Swahili – eBay immediately set up stall around the world, with sites in China, France, Germany, Italy and Japan. And where there were already classifieds sites, like Barcelona's **LoQUo.com** and the Pom/Aussie **Gumtree.com**, it bought them.

Rent.com

A far smoother collaboration has been with **Rent.com**, the US's most popular website for anyone renting, leasing or looking for a roommate. Just in time for Christmas 2004, eBay handed over $415 million (£214 million) to acquire the company and – following the investment in Craigslist – got another foothold in the online property market.

It's easy to see how Rent.com made a success of itself. For a start it's not blighted by the banner ads and pop-ups of other rental and housing sites. It's loaded in the favour of renters, who pay no fees for searching, or posting ads for roommates. All properties are free to view, with floor plans, photos and direct access to phone numbers of landlords. They also have the very alluring offer of $100 cash-in-hand to anyone that can prove they found their current property through the site. For landlords, it's pitched as "no-risk advertising" as – unlike eBay – there are no listings fees. You just have to pay a fee every time a room is taken by a Rent.com user.

What with Craigslist's property listings, and the general upswing in renting versus buying, the acquisition seemed pretty natural. "eBay is once again squaring off directly with the newspaper industry", observed technology blog **Buzzhit!** (buzzhit.com/buzzblog.html), "most notably with **Classified Ventures** – a joint venture of **Gannett**, **Tribune**, **Knight Ridder**, **Belo**, **McClatchy** and *The Washington Post* – which runs **Apartments.com**, **Cars.com** and **Homescape**."

Gumtree

Craigslist is the best for classified ads in the US but when it comes to the UK, the de facto website is **Gumtree**. Founded in March 2000, it's now the UK's most popular website for posting classifieds, and often charts in the top twenty websites in the UK overall, according to alexa.com/topsites. Its focus is on property, so if you are looking for a **flat-share**, or a **tenant**, this is the place. It's also a very popular site for posting **job adverts**, especially for freelancers and part-time vacancies.

Having started off with its focus on London, there's now a Gumtree sub-site for just about every UK city, as well as sixty countries around the world. More than 25,000 new rooms are advertised on the site every month, so Gumtree estimates that their site leads to at least 10,000 rooms being successfully rented every four weeks. Oh, and the most important point: Gumtree is completely free to use. Posting an ad is free, as is replying. And there's no commission to pay either.

10

Freecycle

It's Better Than Binning It!

While most of the sites covered so far are about selling for profit and buying at a discount, one new, fast-growing Internet system takes things ten stages further. Freecycle started off in Tuscon, Arizona, in 2003 when founder Deron Beal sent out a simple email to a few dozen friends and local non-profit organizations listing his unwanted goods that were looking for a new home. His idea was simple: don't throw it away, recycle it. Don't sell it, Freecycle it.

It's not a web platform, or a trading system like eBay or Amazon Marketplace. **Freecycle** exists as a simple concept – you give away what you don't want, and ask around for things that you do want. Signing up is free, and the listings appear by email through a regular newsletter. It sounds great in principle, but then having a policed platform like eBay does have its merits, not least being able to see how trustworthy your fellow users are, and what their history is on the site.

But, in the spirit of Freecycle … nothing ventured nothing gained. If you're not already a member, the first job of any frugal liver is to sign up to their local **TFN** (aka **The Freecycle Network**), which tend to be hosted on **Yahoo! Groups** (groups.yahoo.com), a free communities/forum system. Get a feel for what's available, who's in your local group, and what you could get out of it. And what you could put into it.

Chapter 10

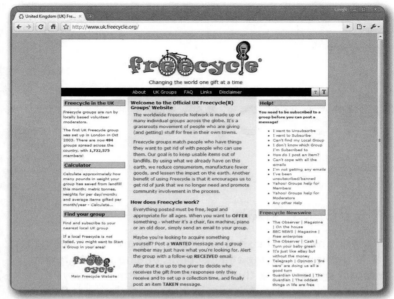

You'll be in good company. By early 2006, there were two million Freecyclers worldwide. And by the summer of 2008 this had grown to **five and half million users worldwide**, across four and half thousand local groups. The local groups aspect is key. Just like the motto at Craigslist, Freecycle is about dealing with people in your local area, helping out your neighbours, and increasing your own town's recycle-to-dump ratio. It's also about **trading safely** with people you can see face to face, as opposed to faceless email contacts.

Freecyclers aren't particularly chatty on their Yahoo! Groups. They tend to cut to the chase and always head up their emails with one of four words (or risk the wrath of their local moderator): *offer*, *taken*, *wanted* or *received*. This is how you need to talk to fit straight in and start getting the most out of the site. Or rather, this is how you need to set out the subject lines of your emails, each followed with a short description of the goods, such as "banjo" or "antique clogs", and then your location.

So if you have something you'd like to get rid of, you send an *offer* email. You then get (hopefully) a whole load of replies from interested parties, which are normally answered on a first-come-first-served basis. You arrange for someone to pop round and pick up your stuff and, when they have and all is well, you post a *taken* email back to the group (maybe with a note on how it all panned out) so everyone knows it went well. Similarly, the lucky recipient will often post a *received* email, to thank the seller.

That just leaves the *wanted* emails. If you're looking for something, try posting a *wanted* ad for it on Freecycle. But look out for, and avoid, the chancers and blaggers – you'll spot them easily enough, busily posting *wanted* notes for laptops, or flat-screen TVs!

In fact it's Freecycle's facility to post free *wanted* ads to people who are – by and large – up for giving, sharing and recycling that often brings out the worst in people. *Has Freecycle turned into a nasty greedfest?* is a regular thread on **mumsnet.com**, with user *Qally* giving an example in spring 2009 that would ring true with most users. "I once saw a long, extremely detailed and well written Freecycle request", she says, "for a Dualit toaster. Which are over a hundred quid in John Lewis. And they lived in a staggeringly expensive area, too. Really seemed to be taking the p****, that one!"

Freecycle Savings

What can you save by Freecycling? *The Guardian* newspaper sums it up perfectly in their handy *Five Quick Calls (Or Clicks) To Save You £1,000+* guide at guardian.co.uk/money/2008/jun/15/consumeraffairs1. "If you are prepared to accept other people's cast-offs (and they can be surprisingly good), the savings (on Freecycle) can be enormous", they report. "Just as importantly, you are saving the planet. Freecycle estimates that by finding new homes for old goods, it saves around 300 tonnes of material going into landfill every day."

And their sister paper, *The Observer*, suggested Freecycle in the run-up to Christmas 2007 as a way of doing the right thing with some of the millions of unwanted Christmas presents that are given every year. "According to research by eBay and YouGov", said their reporter Jon Robins, "we spend £31 on average per gift but more than a third of us (34 percent) can't even remember what our partners bought us last year, let alone anyone else." Read more at guardian .co.uk/money/2007/dec/23/consumeraffairs.christmas2007.

Journalist Liz Phillips went one better for the UK's *Daily Mail* in the run-up to Christmas 2008 when her *So What Can You Do With Those Not-So-Perfect Presents? Return To Santa!* covered not only Freecycle but two other equally worthy and useful alternatives: **SnaffleUp.co.uk** and **Jumbleaid.com**. Read all about it at dailymail.co.uk/money/article-1100976/So-perfect-presents-Return-Santa.html.

Get Started

Head to freecycle.org where you can type in your town or county and find out where the nearest **Freecycle Group** – or **Chapter**, as they like to call them – is to you. While there, check out their **Freecyclopedia** (freecycle .org/freecyclopedia) which covers everything you need to know about the project. Or sit back and watch their instructional video at freecycle.org/ thefreecyclenetwork.swf. In the UK, head to uk.freecycle.org for more local- ized info. Having started up six months after the US, there are now **1.7 million Freecyclers registered in the UK**, across almost five hundred local groups.

11

Satisfaction Guaranteed

The Practicalities Of Selling Online, No Matter What Platform You Use

No matter what platform you choose to sell your goods online, you automatically become thrust into the world of customer service. You want your customers to go away feeling happy because they might buy from you again. And the last thing you want to do is treat them shabbily because, in online sales more than any other walk of life, disgruntled customers are very quick to speak up. I've used this chapter to compile tips on everything from making sure your goods get to their destination in one piece, to how to get your ever-expanding customer base hankering for more.

Shipping Tips

No matter what site you're using to sell your stuff to raise some cash, the onus is always is on you, the seller, to manage the logistics of getting the item to your buyer safe and sound, even though it's the buyer's job to cover the costs. And that's the first thing a good seller needs to consider. What will the shipping costs be? How will the item be shipped? Will it go through the mail or a courier service? Thinking this all through early on can help you **make the most profit** but it can also actually **help you sell your item**. Research has shown that buyers who are upfront and detailed about their shipping costs are more likely to make a sale than those that aren't.

Amazon calculates the shippings costs and adds a mark-up for you. And on eBay there are tools within the **Sell Your Item** form to help you calculate what your shipping costs might be. You can either choose a **flat rate**, or have it calculated **based on the buyer's address**. US sellers have a whole host of

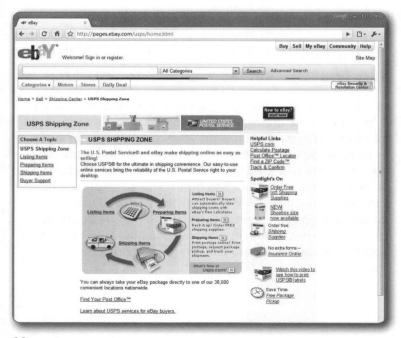

Four Quick Shipping Tips

1 Don't be tempted to inflate your shipping costs to make extra money Buyers see through this and, chances are, someone else is selling something similar and asking for a reasonable postage fee, so they'll buy from them instead.

2 Put some time and effort into packaging your items up well The last thing you want after taking the time and trouble to list, auction and sell something online is for it to get damaged on the way to the winning buyer. They'll most likely take action against you and it will show up in your feedback ratings. The best advice is to spend every last penny of the shipping fee you charge on making sure the item is safely and properly packed.

3 Be realistic about weight If you're planning to sell a set of dumb bells, light aircraft, or something equally heavy, check the Freight Resource Centre at ebay .freightquote.com to find out how many stamps you'll need. Eurotunnel had to in April 2004 when they set up one of eBay's heaviest ever auctions, to sell off the 580-tonne drill they'd used to build the Channel Tunnel!

4 Pack it right From "loosefill peanuts" to "encapsulated air plastic sheeting" (that's bubble-wrap to you and me), UPS provides a detailed inventory of every possible packaging option known to mankind. Go to ups.com, click **Support**, then **Preparing Your Package**.

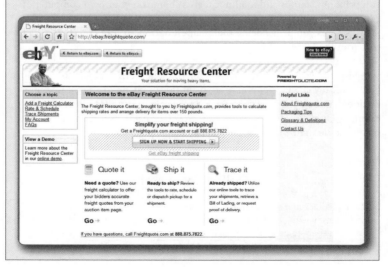

facilities as a result of a tie-up between eBay and the **United States Postal Service**. You can enter size and weight details into a shipping price calculator, print address labels, log pick-up requests and also get free flat-rate shipping boxes via ebay.com/usps. **DHL**, **FedEx** and **UPS** all have similar offerings.

Online postage services are less sophisticated in the UK, though there is a **Print Postage Label** system built into **eBay** that lets you pay for mailing with **PayPal** and print everything you need at home. Royal Mail (royalmail .com) does offer a postcode checking system, and its **SmartStamp** service lets you print out stamps and mailing labels at home on your own computer. It's expensive though, with a £49.99 per year subscription (plus however many SmartStamps you print) being the cheapest option. (There's no such start-up cost with the USPS system.)

Scissors, wrapping paper, bubble-wrap, boxes and Jiffy bags are also something to consider at this stage – all available from **Post Offices** of course but, ironically, in cheaper and more plentiful supply online. Look in eBay's **Business, Office & Industrial > Packing & Posting Supplies** category, for example. Or, alternatively, ask on Freecycle (see p.93), as it is amazing how many people want to get shot of such stuff.

Online Calculator

There's a quick and easy shipping cost calculator on **UPS**'s main website. Just type where you're sending from and to and it will give you an idea of the costs you can expect to be dealing with. Find it at servicecenter.ups.com/ebay/ebay .html and scroll down to **UPS Rates and Services**.

Customs Costs

What might cost you – or your buyer – more are **customs fees and import taxes** if you're shipping to another country. Whatever country you ship from the customs declaration forms you'll fill in for international sales are pretty much the same. The one thing that people get stuck on is the item type and the value. You get four choices of item type: **Gift**, **Commercial Sample**, **Documents** or **Other**. While most people tick Gift hoping that customs fees will be avoided, this is technically against the law, and could land you (and your buyer) in hot water. In the **Value** box you need to enter the final sale price of the item. Play it straight – don't include shipping fees and don't enter the price you originally paid for the item or what you think the market value might be. The value of the item in question is simple – whatever the buyer chose to pay for it. And to make this perfectly clear, it's a simple but very effective idea to **include a print-out** of the final item listing when you post any item, whether it's internationally or just around the corner.

Customer Satisfaction

When people moan about the death of customer service in the era of mass-market and impersonal corporations, online sales sites are going some way toward changing things. After all, you're not buying anything from them, or from a company, you're **buying from an individual**. And that gives a chance for good old customer service to come back into fashion. Besides, if you make one sale and you plan to make more, the happier you keep your buyers, the higher your **feedback ratings** will be and the more sales you can make.

There are several points you can put in your item listing – no matter what platform you use – that will generate some warm feelings among your browsers, and help turn them into buyers. State your **returns or warranty policy** clearly, perhaps offering a **money-back guarantee** if the buyer is not satisfied. You could also offer special deals on shipping – like discounts for multiple item purchases – or provide a gift-wrapping option. You might also decide to **donate a percentage of the final sale price to charity**. The more they bid, the more you donate.

The most reassuring listings to read are often those with a strong set of **Q&As** between the seller and potential buyers. Then, once the item's been bagged, customers will always be happier if you contact them immediately, remind them of shipping costs and payment options and fill them in on the next stage. The longer you leave it, the longer it will be until you see your money and, as with anything bought online (i.e., not face to face), the buyer needs continual nudging to get them to part with their cash.

When you have the money (in eBay's case, as you're paid immediately on Amazon Marketplace), the best feedback will be generated if you **despatch the goods as quickly as possible** and – as mentioned above – **as well packaged as you can**. Send an email confirmation at the same time to say it's on its way. Another way to get good feedback, and get customers returning, is to include a little surprise in the package. If the item you're selling takes batteries, perhaps include some if they're not too expensive. Or perhaps throw in a photo, a postcard, or some sweets. Nothing that will break the bank but just a token that says "thanks for buying from me, and not the other one hundred million sellers out there"!

12

Trading Safely

Dangerous Emails, Identity Theft And Bogus websites

While buying and selling online is becoming increasingly more secure, and better policed, it would be wrong to think of it as a completely risk-free activity. All computer users are familiar with spam and, at its most passive, spam tries to sell you things – anything from Viagra to tea kettles. But at its most intrusive and destructive, spam can contain viruses or phishing systems. Such emails purport to be from a legitimate source, luring you to a fake webpage where you are asked to provide personal and financial details. Phishing emails are important to look out for as they often purport to be from the main companies covered in this book: Amazon, Verizon, PayPal, eBay and many of the major US and UK banks and credit card companies.

Chapter 12

Phishing Fears

Why is it called **phishing**? According to **PrivacyRights.org**, it's because "Individuals who 'bite' are exposed to identity theft". The first criminal to be convicted of such a practice in the UK was a 29-year-old whose gang stole £200,000. "They set up a network of computers which sent out emails to eBay customers asking for their details", explained **BBC News**. "People who replied thought they were taken to a secure eBay site when they were in fact connected to the criminals' own computers … Using these stolen credentials the gang would then access the accounts of vendors with a reliable, recommended sales history and assume their identity. The gang would then offer expensive items up for sale, such as laptop computers and designer watches, before disappearing with the cash."

At almost exactly the same time, over in Arizona, someone was prosecuted for stealing the identities of various Phoenix residents, with which

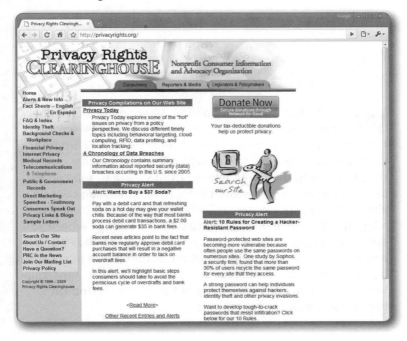

fake PayPal accounts were created and cars bought on eBay. Going one stage further, other phishing scams have lured Internet users into providing their **personal bank details and PIN numbers**, so criminals can simply access their accounts and withdraw money.

Many Internet Service Providers attempt to safeguard Web and eBay users against phishing. **Hotmail** (hotmail.com) will warn you if a sender's ID could not be verified. And **EarthLink** (earthlink.net), an ISP service designed specifically for eBay users, has its own **ScamBlocker** system. But note that phishing emails can be well camouflaged and might contain legitimate companies' names in the "From" field (a surprisingly easy thing to set up) and they **often contain the real companies' logos and graphics**. Falling into such a scam is nothing to be ashamed of, as most of them actually prey on Internet users' fears of identity theft in order to get them to part with their personal details. This is why many dangerous emails are headed up "Please Update Your Details" or "Urgent Account Update". Take a look overleaf at a typical example of a fraudulent email:

Subject: eBay Account Verification
Date: Fri, 20 Jun 2009 07:38:39 -0700
From: "eBay" <accounts@ebay.com>
Reply-To: accounts@ebay.com

Dear eBay member,
As part of our continuing commitment to protect your account and to reduce the instance of fraud on our website, we will undertaking a period review of our member accounts.
You are requested to visit our site by following the link goven below:
http://slp.clinker.net.mx/.it/.x/index.htm?SignIn&ssPageName
Please fill in the required information.
This is required for us to continue to offer you a safe and risk free environment to send and receive money online, and maintain the eBay Experience.
Thank you

Accounts Management As outlined in our User Agreement, eBay will periodically send you information about site changes and enhancements. Visit our Privacy Policy and User Agreement if you have any questions.
Copyright © 1995-2009 eBay Inc. All Rights Reserved.
Designated trademarks and brands are the property
of their respective owners.
Use of this Web site constitutes acceptance of the eBay User Agreement and Privacy Policy.

How do you know such an email is fake? Try this checklist:

1 Don't click that link It doesn't even contain the name **eBay** and **.mx** (Mexico) is nowhere near eBay's headquarters.

2 eBay and PayPal always send emails addressing the user by name They would never include such phrases as "Dear Valued Customer".

3 Check your email headers Take a look at the email headers in your mail application or webmail site to see if the email really is from **accounts@ebay .com** as it purports.

4 Look for bad English The examples here being "link goven below"? and "We will undertaking". No official email would ever include such grammatical errors or spelling mistakes.

5 Why is the matter so urgent? There is never any urgency about updating your account details on eBay, so don't be fooled that there is.

6 Don't place too much stock in the header and footer That includes the eBay logo and legal small print; they've just been copied straight off a legitimate eBay message.

7 Be suspicious of timed warnings The 72-hour warning is not something to take seriously – no reputable online business would ever issue such a deadline.

8 Your PIN is always your own Remember that no official business would ever ask you to enter your credit or debit card PIN number, as phishing sites and emails often do. In fact, few will ever email asking you to verify your personal details, a line that should immediately cause suspicion.

9 Is it a secure page? If you do open a link in a suspicious email, make sure the page it takes you to begins with **https://**, not **http://**. The **s** stands for **secure**, and official pages would always contain this. Only ever open a link if you have reason to think an email might be genuine – just by clicking on it could open you up to a virus attack.

None of these are completely foolproof ways of spotting a bogus email. So if you are ever in doubt, there is one vital way to check if an email you have received really is from who it claims to be. Just log into your account and check your **Messages** page there. If your suspicious email arrives as a new message there, then go ahead and deal with it. If it's not there, do one thing and one thing only – **delete it**. As eBay say themselves, "(the) My Messages (section) is the definitive, legitimate source for any email from eBay that affects your account. The bottom line – if an email affects your eBay account, it's in **My Messages**."

The various phishing blogs are useful places to keep track of new threats and compare emails you are suspicious of with those the bloggers have tracked themselves. bankersonline.com/phishing, mailchannels .blogspot.com, onlinefraud.blogspot.com and the more academic indiana .edu/~phishing/blog are all worth a look. eBay's own anti-phishing guide, the **Spoof (Fake) Emails Tutorial**, can be found at pages.ebay.com/education/ spooftutorial.

Chapter 12

If The Worst Happens

Forward planning is the best form of security online, but if you have given out your personal details, or you believe your security has been breached, these are the steps you should take:

1 Forward the phishing email to the business it claimed to be from For **eBay**, forward the email to spoof@ebay.com. There's no need to write an accompanying email but if you want to go into more depth go to **Help > Contact Us > Account Security** and fill in the form. Similarly, bogus **PayPal** emails can be sent to spoof@paypal.com.

2 Check your system for viruses Nearly all viruses are aimed at PC users, so use a virus scanner such as those available from the **Norton** brand (symantec.com) and **AVG** (free.avg.com), the latter being free. Norton also sell virus protection software for Apple Macs, though you might do better to spend your money on an external backup device and use OS X's **Time Machine** software to restore your system if you run into problems. Whether you use a Mac or a Windows PC, always try to keep your operating system and browser software up to date as a first line of defence.

3 Change your password immediately Make sure it's unique, and never use the same password for Hotmail, PayPal, eBay or other websites you regularly use.

Learn More...

You can learn more about phishing from these organizations, all of which are fighting to stamp it out:

- ▶ **Anti-Phishing Working Group** antiphishing.org
- ▶ **Better Business Bureau** bbb.org/phishing
- ▶ **Federal Trade Commission** ftc.gov/bcp/conline/publs/alerts/phishingalrt.htm
- ▶ **Phishing Info** phishinginfo.org
- ▶ **Wise Geek** wisegeek.com

4 Report your incident Get on the phone and tell your bank and/or credit card company immediately...

Panic Stations For eBay Users

If you think your eBay account may have been tampered with, report it immediately by chatting live with an **official representative**. You'll find a link to do this at pages.ebay.com/help/confidence/isgw-account-theft-reporting .html. You should also regularly check their **Security Centre**. It's not too easy to find, though, and the consumer group **Which?** in the UK (where more than a hundred eBay-related crimes are reported to the Metropolitan Police every month) has long been calling for it to be better signposted. It's in the **Marketplace Safety** section of **Community**. Click to it direct at pages.ebay .com/securitycenter.

Intermediate and professional users should also make time to browse the **Law Enforcement Centre** at pages.ebay.com/securitycenter/ law_enforcement.html where they'll find information on eBay's **Fraud Investigation Team** (FIT). If you are working with your local police force to investigate a **cybercrime**, point them to this page as it has all the email addresses and phone numbers they need to deal with the appropriate eBay officials. Anyone more than a casual eBay user would do well to stop off at the **Trust & Safety (SafeHarbor) Discussion Board**. This is the main place to discuss and flag up fraudulent and illegal activity and you can get there via **Community > Security & Resolution Center > Trust & Safety (Safe Harbor)**. It's a hotbed of crime and intrigue with topics such as "auction interference", "possible Chinese laptop fraud" and "Xbox 360 pre-order fraud" being regular areas of debate.

Part 4:
Savings & Freebies

13

Comparison Sites

...For Cheaper Insurance And Best-Value Personal Finance

Price comparison websites started to spring up in the late 1990s, evolving out of the "virtual shopping malls" that were set up to pool together the rapidly emerging hordes of online shops. In the ten years that have followed they have grown in sophistication to such a point that, if you're buying car insurance for example, it's far quicker and easier to find the best deal on a comparison site than by searching for a new policy in the press, by phone or by trawling Google.

All the key comparison sites are free to use. They make their money from the businesses they list (who either pay them a flat insertion fee, or a token amount every time you click through from the comparison site to theirs). So can you really use them to save money? Definitely. According to **GoCompare. com**, 52 percent of their customers make savings on their car insurance by using their system.

The Big Guns

Price comparison websites vary in popularity and specialism from the US to the UK. They're massive in the US in two main areas: for **travel** (and related purchases such as hotels) and **shopping** (entertainment, electrical goods, fashion and beauty etc). In the UK, on the other hand, they're less well-known for shopping (although they still have a huge and dedicated user-base) in favour of **anything finance-related**, from insurance to gas bills.

Confused.com

Confused.com was the first insurance comparison website to appear in the UK and is by far the most well known. Back in 2002 it covered only **car insurance** but in 2005 they added **home insurance** and now, in 2009, their search service is comprehensive to say the least. It covers all areas of **insurance** (life, home and travel, as well as car, van, motorbike and breakdown), **money** (credit cards, personal loans, mortgages, and ISAs), and **utilities** (gas, electricity, TV, broadband and phone).

They make their money every time you buy insurance from one of their listed companies. So that means they don't earn money from insurers paying

Chapter 13

Moneysupermarket.com

The longest running of the UK comparison sites, **Moneysupermarket.com** first launched in 1999. At that time it covered only mortgages but, in 2000, it added credit card and personal loan comparisons and, in 2003, launched the **Travelsupermarket.com** spin-off. The website was initially started by university student Simon Nixon (still a visible force on the website) and his girlfriend's brother, Duncan Cameron. Do these comparison websites make money? Well in 2007 Cameron sold his half of the business to Nixon... for £162 million.

to be listed, and can thus provide an impartial service. It also means, of course, that you could use Confused.com to do your research, and then phone the insurer or bank you've chosen to apply direct; as you might expect, they urge you not to, and there really is no benefit in not following through from them.

Their site tracks 86 car insurance providers, 63 home insurers and 35 travel insurers. So it would be crazy to get quotes direct when you can get comparative fees and save yourself time and money in the process. There's a full list of all of the insurers Confused.com works with at confused.com/providers.

GoCompare.com

When it comes to insurance specifically for your car, the main website to check is **GoCompare.com**. Launched in November 2006, it was founded by an insurance specialist, Hayley Parsons, and was the first UK price compari-

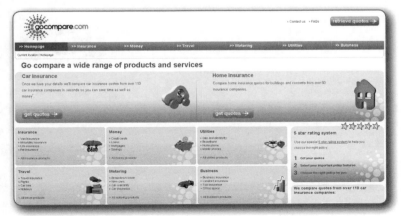

Which To Choose?

But which to choose, when **GoCompare.com** and **Confused.com** offer such similar services? In short, use GoCompare.com for car insurance as they track 100 insurers as opposed to Confused.com's 86. And use Confused for your home insurance as they examine 63 different companies versus GoCompare.com's 50. And for pretty much everything else, go to GoCompare.com first as they track various other financial services their competitors do not, such as business insurance, mobile phones and current accounts.

---

son site to compare and contrast competing insurers by their features and benefits, as opposed to just listing by price and highlighting the cheapest. In 2008, it became the first comparison site to join the British Insurance Brokers Association (BIBA) and, like Confused.com, has since added **travel insurance**, **life insurance** and all manner of other annual expenses.

Interpreting The Results

Each of the price comparison sites has its own dedicated user-base but, if you're new to this area of saving money online, it's best to have a quick try of each and find out which is quickest and easiest for you personally to get to grips with. Certainly **GoCompare.com** has the simplest and easiest interface to navigate. But then **Moneysupermarket.com** has a wealth of **community input**, **forums** and **Q&As** that most of the other sites lack. They've also got case studies of users who have tackled the quagmire of mobile phone contracts, switching gas supplier or whatever and come out the other side with better deals and more spare cash in their pocket.

The No-Shows

One thing you mustn't forget – and many insurers won't let you, with their regular TV ads – is that there are some notable companies missing from all the major comparison sites. **Direct Line** has been the most vocal anti-comparison company in the UK. "Direct Line, the insurer, has launched a stinging attack on online price comparison services", reported *The Daily Telegraph* as far back as 2007, "claiming that they are not accurate, independent or comprehensive". You can read more at telegraph.co.uk/finance/personalfinance/

Chapter 13

insurance/2810337/Direct-line-takes-a-swat-at-best-buys.html. One site, **Moneysupermarket.com**, is very upfront about who they don't include. At moneysupermarket.com/c/customer-promise/companies-not-compared/ they list **NatWest**, **Tesco**, **RBS**, **Nationwide** and various others that have opted out of their system for one reason or another. *The Guardian* tackled Direct Line on the subject in their *Beware When You Compare* article, which is well worth a read, at guardian.co.uk/money/2007/jun/22/insurance.

A Pinch Of Salt?

While comparison sites are useful, don't expect them to do all the work for you. In the summer of 1999, *Which?* magazine sent its researchers off to get quotes across six comparison websites. Amazingly they found that "all of the

---

Real-Life Savings

By working through the various sections of Moneysupermarket.com, Emma Thone, 36, from Bristol saved £580 off her domestic running costs. That's £109 on her home insurance premium, £159 per year off her gas and electricity, £120 by switching mobile phone provider, and £190 by switching banks for her current account. The website has numerous other, equally inspiring real-life stories at moneysupermarket.com/c/news-and-community, like Glasgow-based couple David and Karien Pirie who saved £500 off their total annual costs with a similar web-based financial makeover. But the biggest saver of any comparison site shopper has to be Richard Keeble, 60, from Kingston-upon-Thames who managed to save £7500 from his annual costs. You can read his story at moneysupermarket.com/c/news/money-makeover-is-richard-the-countrys-best-money-saver/0004989/.

---

sites failed as one-stop-shops, as none consistently gave the cheapest quote", and "different websites sometimes gave different quotes for the same insurer". You can find out more about their research at which.co.uk/advice/price-comparison-sites/is-the-price-right. The moral? Use a comparison site to get a feel for the market and see what deals are out there, don't treat the results as definitive, and don't forget to check the companies that opt out.

Comparing The Comparison Sites

The only way to get a true handle on the price comparison sites is to, well, compare them all. **Moneysupermarket.com** is the most proactive in this area. In 2008 they took the ten most searched-for products on their site and checked to see which service offered the biggest choice of providers. On savings accounts they came out top, comparing 69 banks. **Moneyextra.com**, **Moneyfacts** (moneyfacts.co.uk) and **uSwitch** (uswitch.com) all came a close second with 68.

For home insurance, they obtained quotes for buildings and contents

Chapter 13

Comparing Inside With Outside

Many of the personal finance sites (see p.112) cover home contents insurance. But one thing you need to make sure of is that your policy includes the contents that you take out and about every day. Especially as, in this post-Walkman, iPod-, iPhone-crazy era, people are carrying a small fortune of gadgets in their pockets as soon as they leave the house. One of the comparison sites, **Tescocompare.com**, say they urge people to "take a closer look at what is hiding in their bags and pockets and consider what would happen if these items were lost or stolen..."

According to the UK government's 2008 *British Crime Survey* (homeoffice .gov.uk/rds/pdfs09/personal_theft_0708.xls), **the average total value of the possessions we carry around with us comes to £173 per person.**

insurance for a 35-year-old married male living in a three-bedroom semi-detached house with a market value of £200,000 and contents worth £40,000. Moneysupermarket.com had 58 companies on file, with **Confused.com** and **GoCompare.com** coming in at 54 each. **Comparethemarket.com** had 32 and Tesco's own **Tescocompare.com** just 20. You can read the full breakdown of Moneysupermarket.com's useful research at moneysupermarket.com/c/customer-promise/comprehensive-service.

The Male/Female Comparison

Swiftcover.com offers car, travel and pet insurance online, and trumpets the fact that they are Britain's only insurance company without call centres, which means that the resulting cost savings can be passed directly onto the customer and premiums are kept low.

In 2008 Swiftcover.com was featured on **Moneysupermarket.com** more than any other insurer as the cheapest on the market. And they've got a thing or two to say about the male/female divide on the road, revealing that male drivers accounted for more than half of the total car insurance claim costs of 2008, despite actually making fewer than half of the claims. They also found that:

1 Men are twice as likely to speed in a 30mph zone.

2 Men are three times more likely to speed on motorways and rural roads.

3 Men are four times more likely to be convicted of speeding offences.

4 Men are nine times more likely to be convicted of driving offences.

Tesco came out low in all comparative searches but they are well worth using if you need to get a good deal on insurance for **niche cars**. Their site is the only comparison site with clear links and sections for owners of classic cars, 4x4s and kit cars. Our advice? For a clear, easy-to-use experience, go to **GoCompare.com**. For support, background info and forums, the best is **Moneysupermarket.com**. For anything automotive, the best is **Confused .com**. For mortgages, shares and finance news, try **Motley Fool** (fool.co.uk). And for travel insurance, the AA's specialist travel site **QuoteBanana.co.uk** is well worth a look.

14

Comparison Shopping

...For The Best Prices And Best Value On Domestic Goods

While price comparison sites focusing on insurance and personal finance are more popular in the UK and Europe than the US, the spread of popularity of comparison sites that cover more general day-to-day shopping is far more even. In this chapter we'll take a look at the cream of the comparison crop.

US Sites

Deal Scans

Deal Scans (dealscans.com) is a simple example. It automatically scans 23 well-known stores across a variety of products and displays a chart showing who's the cheapest and by how much. All the big names are covered, from **Best Buy** to **Walmart** via **Circuit City** and **Target**. You can browse the chart or search by product, price or store.

Outletscanner

They've also come up with a spin-off software app, **Outletscanner** (outletscanner.com), which scans the **Dell Outlet Store** (dell.com/outlet and dell.co.uk/outlet) for products and bargains that match the exact spec of the PC you're looking to buy and finds the cheapest possible price.

Smarter.com

A luxury version of Deal Scans comes in the form of **Smarter.com**, which adds numerous shopping blogs and video reviews from users. Founded in 2002 (and becoming the number four price comparison site a few years later), it searches 21 stores including **BuyAndWalk .com**, **OverstockDrugstore .com**, **iGearUSA.com** and **GiftCollector.com**. Smarter.com also has **Canadian** (smarter.com.  cn) and **Japanese** (smarter.co.jp) sister sites and competes head-on with **Shopzilla**, which has an equivalent service, if a more boring and less interactive web presence across the **US** (shopzilla.com), **UK** (shopzilla.co.uk), **France** (shopzilla.fr) and **Germany** (shopzilla.de).

Chapter 14

Külist

Külist (kulist.com) originates from California and adds a few interesting twists of its own. First up, it compares prices for all manner of household goods across sites such as **Google Products**, **Become.com**, **Shopping.com**, **PriceGrabber**, **Shopzilla**, **PriceRunner**, **Buy.com**, **Bestprices** and **J&R**. But it does so "on the fly". You install the Külist bookmark bar, it sits in your browser and when you spot a product you fancy, you drag it to the Külist bar to get some prices.

They also offer a cashback service on some products and sites. How? Well Külist takes a referral fee every time you buy something via their service, and they pass a cut of it back to you. **TechCrunch** delivered an in-depth review of the site (techcrunch.com/2006/06/15/kulist-offers-price-comparison-bookmarklet-and-cash-back) when it launched and, as their reviewer said, "It may not be pretty, but I like the way it works."

Dealtagger & Priceheat

Dealtagger (dealtagger.com) and **Priceheat** (priceheat .com) offer similar toolbar-based apps. Priceheat is the one for decent **Safari** and **Firefox** integration, and you can take a quick guided tour of Dealtagger's features at dealtagger.com/help/tour.

UK Sites

In the UK, **PriceRunner**, **Kelkoo** and **PriceGrabber** are the three main sites vying to replace the time and energy you'd traditionally spend trawling the High Street comparing one shop with another while on the hunt for anything from a new toaster to new shoes.

PriceRunner

Unlike any other, **PriceRunner** (pricerunner.co.uk), which has been going for more than ten years, claims to have a team of people on the ground, working shop floors gathering real-life price data, as opposed to taking automated feeds from other websites.

Kelkoo

Kelkoo (kelkoo.co.uk) is by far the biggest, though, and the most popular. Founded in 2000 (and having absorbed other big comparison sites like **Zoomit** and **Shopgenie**), it's the largest e-commerce site in Europe (after **Amazon** and **eBay**, of course) and the largest online advertising platform in Europe. The stats are impressive: Kelkoo tracks more than three million products, brands from Apple to Aston Martin, and works with 41 of the UK's

---

Top Twenty Comparisons

What stores can you compare on the product-focused comparison sites? These are the top ten most popular – as judged by products bought on Kelkoo UK – from the first three months of 2009.

1 Amazon

2 Amazon Marketplace

3 eBay

4 Dell

5 Price Minister (priceminister.co.uk)

6 Play.com

7 Very.co.uk

8 Pixmania (pixmania.co.uk)

9 Screwfix (screwfix.com)

10 Boots Kitchen Appliances (bootskitchenappliances.co.uk)

Chapter 14

top 50 retailers. Which means there's very little point in going to the websites or physical stores of **Argos**, **Carphone Warehouse**, **GAME** or various other High Street names. You might as well just compare their prices by going to Kelkoo straight off.

PriceGrabber

Though not the largest of the UK's comparison sites, **PriceGrabber** (pricegrabber.co.uk) arguably gets the prize for cleanest look and feel. The specialized "Fashion" and "Gadget" blogs within the site are especially useful features. And for those on the other side of the pond, there's also an American branch (pricegrabber.com).

Specialist Sites

For dedicated comparison shoppers, there's a host of nice sites out there covering everything from **antique books** to **car parks**. Here's a round-up of some of the best market-specific comparison sites, and the niches they service…

Compare Books

For comparing book prices, the most popular by far is **BookFinder** (bookfinder.com) but the friendliest site has to be **Lovereading**. Their Book Price Comparison Engine (lovereading.co.uk/comparebookprices.php), they report, allows you to "quickly and easily, be able to compare book and postage prices from over a dozen online book retailers." Other book comparison sites worth checking out include **BooksPrice.co.uk**, which searches 52 separate stores including Amazon Markertplace, Tesco, Asda and Waterstones

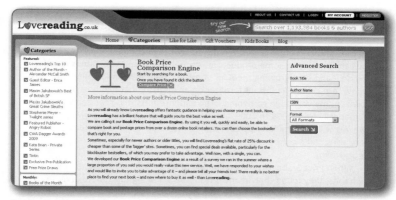

(you can see the full list at booksprice.co.uk/FAQ.jsp). Try **BookFly** (bookfly
.co.uk) for the smoothest user interface or, for a good selection of US stores,
BookFinder4u.com scans 130 outlets.

Compare Airport Parking

If you're in the UK and plan on flying from **Stansted Airport** in the near
future, first point your browser at compare-airport-parking.co.uk. "We compare over 1,000 prices from the biggest providers every day", they claim.
There's an equally useful site covering 35 **Gatwick Airport** car parks at
airport-parking-shop.co.uk/gatwick/gatwick-airport-parking.html, and **Go
Simply** covers almost every UK airport at gosimply.com/airport-parking.
There isn't really an equivalent in the US, but **LongTermParking.com** pools
info on all the main airports from Alabama to Washington with price info
and discount coupons.

Comparing Hotels

The basic (but very well specified) **Hotel Prices Compare** is worth a look.
Type hotelpricescompare.com, and enter your destination to automatically
compare hotels from up to thirty booking sites such as **InterContinental.com**,
HotelBook.com, **LateRooms.com** and **ReserveTravel.com**. But as with all
comparison sites – especially travel-related – do your own research (online
and offline) to back up the good deals you'll find.

The mother of all room-booking websites is the perfectly monikered
Booking.com. They cover more than 15,000 destinations, survey 68,000

Chapter 14

hotels and claim more than 100,000 room nights are booked through them every day. Down under, the Australian **Hotels Combined** (hotelscombined .com) has a wide selection in certain top destinations (588 hotels just in Venice, for example) and thrives on user reviews. For various UK regional hotels, **Hotels Comparison** (hotelscomparison.com) is revered, and was voted the best hotels comparison website by *The Sunday Times*.

Compare Music

There are two massive websites for comparing prices on second-hand music and vinyl, but their history is slightly different to the other sites in this chapter. Instead of setting out with the consumer in mind, they started off in the early days of the web with the seller in mind, acting as a portal to second-hand stores who couldn't afford to set up their own websites, but who wanted to make their stock – and prices – available online. Step forward **GEMM.com** in the US and **Net Sounds** (netsoundsmusic.com) in the UK. Both offer a

Comparison Shopping

sterling service to the seller community and, as a result, a huge price comparison database to buyers. Also take a look at **MusicStack** (musicstack.com) and the dance-focused **VinylSearcher** (vinylsearcher.com).

Compare Driving Lessons

The driving school market has some surprising similarities with second-hand music retail: lots of small providers, with little time or inclination to market themselves online. The perfect target, then, for portals and comparison sites. Three ready-made, location-based driving school comparison sites to try are **UK Driving Schools** (compare-driving-schools.co.uk), **Choosy Learner.com** (choosylearner.com) and **Compare Instructors** (compareinstructors.co.uk).

Compare Cookers

Everyone needs a cooker but they can cost a fortune and they're not exactly available in every High Street. Which makes them perfect price comparison website fodder. In the US, **Pricescan.com** and **Shopping.yahoo.com** will both help you find a good price. And, in the UK, **Compare Store Prices** has a dedicated kitchen and cooker section (comparestoreprices.co.uk/kitchen-appliances. asp) which helped buy your author the very cooker that fueled the writing of this book! Or try **Appliances.co.uk** for a broader range of white goods.

Chapter 14

Compare Cars

If you're looking to buy a new car, many of the generic price comparison websites can help. On **Moneysupermarket.com**, for example, head straight to moneysupermarket.com/new-cars/car-prices.aspx. Then there's the magazine-based and classified ad-based websites such as **Autotrader** (autotrader

.co.uk) and **Auto Express** (autoexpress. co.uk/carreviews/ grouptests). And, bubbling under, there are a few dedicated price comparison sites for new cars such as **CarPriceChecker** (carpricechecker.co.uk) and **Askaprice.com**.

Compare Consoles

The popularity – and high price tag – of the **Nintendo Wii** has brought many specialist comparison sites to the web. They represent the "here today/gone tomorrow" side of comparison shopping where there's very little in it for the buyer. Instead, it's all about the commission the sites get from whoever you eventually click through to buy from. They also try to scrape in some extra income by covering their sites in ads. They're worth a look if only to get your

Top Of The Comps UK

Here are the ten most popular websites for comparison shopping, according to web stats firm **Alexa** (alexa.com). Some are insurance- or finance-based, others more for household shopping or reviews. But this is how they stack up against each other by number of users.

1 Google Products Search (google.co.uk/products)

2 Ciao UK (ciao.co.uk)

3 Moneysupermarket.com (moneysupermarket.com)

4 Shopping.com UK (uk.shopping.com)

5 Kelkoo UK (kelkoo.co.uk)

6 Dooyoo UK (dooyoo.co.uk)

7 NexTag UK (nextag.co.uk)

8 Compare Store Prices UK (comparestoreprices.co.uk)

9 PriceRunner (pricerunner.co.uk)

10 Confused.com (confused.com)

head around what prices you might expect to pay for a console, games or game bundles. Four to try in the UK are **Wiiprices.co.uk**, **CompareWiiFit .co.uk**, **Compare-Wii-Prices.co.uk** and **WiiCompare.com**.

For a variety of consoles, try the rough-and-ready **Compare Console Prices** (compareconsoleprices.co.uk) and the slightly slicker, PlayStation-focused **Playstation4prices.com**, which also runs an email newsletter on the latest deals available.

It's also worth looking at some of the high-profile tech reviews websites for price comparisons. From games to satnav consoles, **TechRadar** is one of the best. Check their **Tom Tom** console price round-up, for example, at techradar.com/reviews/gadgets/tom-tom-gps-and-sat-nav/tomtom-go-740-live-506775/price-comparison.

Compare Wines

The main driving school comparison websites (see p.127) are all UK-based. And the main wine comparison websites are all US-based. Whatever this says about our intercontinental differences should be settled over a glass of claret from the incredibly far-reaching **Wine-Searcher** (wine-searcher.com). As of July 2009 it was listing 14,383 wine stores with 3,919,726 offers between

Chapter 14

them. **WineFetch** (winefetch.com), on the other hand, leads with the bargains available – such as a *2006 Patz & Hall Chardonnay* for $36.99, or an *L. Aubry Fils Brut Champagne* for $48.99. **WineZap** (winezap.com), however, has by far the best user interface, a community approach and various videos (such as the informative *Opening a Wine Bottle Without a Corkscrew* at winezap.com/aboutme/viewFile/1411).

Comparing Odds

If there's one tip guaranteed to save you money it's try not to gamble. But if you're partial to online gambling, there are a few online sites comparing odds from the various bookies. **Betfair** (betfair.com) isn't a comparison site but always has a round-up of the odds its competitors are offering on its home page. **Checkyourodds.co.uk** suffers from a case of information overload, which leaves **Oddschecker.com** as the one to dig into deeply. It covers all sorts of sports from American football to greyhound racing.

15

Saving On Utilities

Heat, Light And The Essentials

Heating, lighting, gas, electricity, water: all vital daily expenses but ones for which you can quite easily overpay. In the UK and, increasingly, in the US, it's possible to compare tariffs across various suppliers and make a quick and easy switch to save some money. There are also various websites providing tips on saving on essential household bills, which we'll come to later in this chapter.

Switching Energy Suppliers

The first big step is to make sure you're getting the cheapest electricity coming through your wires. "Customers who switched gas and electricity (dual fuel) with **Confused.com**", the comparison website claims, "between 1 January 2008 and 31 December 2008 saved on average £252.37." Reason enough to get back on the comparison sites and do for your energy bills what you should have done (if you're reading this book from front to back!) for your insurance premiums.

Chapter 15

It's even more important to make sure you're saving money and getting the best deal in light of the fact that energy bills are increasing, almost exponentially. In 2004, the average **UK household energy bill** was £580. By summer 2009, it had reached £1243, a 114 percent increase. Global demand, price volatility, investment in green initiatives – these are all reasons for the price hike, and none are set to diminish any time soon.

"This is a wake-up call for us all", says Ann Robinson, Director of Consumer Policy at **uSwitch.com**. "The £5000 a year energy bill may seem like an outside possibility, but we have to remember that energy bills doubled in the last five years alone and that the huge investment needed just to keep the lights on in Britain will alone add £548 a year onto our bills. The fact is we are entering a new era of high cost energy and households will have to adapt their behaviour accordingly." We will indeed, but how?

The first thing to do is check what offers your current supplier is providing online. Most offer **special online-only tariffs** that should net you a saving of at least £50. "In addition to being able to change payment details any time you want via your online account, you'll also stop receiving paper bills", explains the **Energy Choices** watchdog. "Instead, you'll be emailed when your payment is due. You'll also have to enter your own meter readings – eliminating the need to wait around for an engineer, or run the risk of overpaying on an estimated bill." (We look at potential overpaying in more depth below.)

Saving On Utilities

The Best Online Tariffs

- **British Gas** You can save at least £100 by switching to British Gas' online-only tariff called Web Saver 3 (britishgas.co.uk).

- **E.ON** Energy Choices reports a possible saving of up to £171 with E.ON's EnergyOnline tariff (eonenergy.com).

- **Npower** Appropriately for the Ashes sponsor, Npower offers a £192 saving right off the bat, although the dreaded "terms and conditions apply" (Npower.com).

- **Scottish Power** Scottish Power's so-called green energy tariffs come in three different flavours (scottishpower.co.uk).

- **Utilita** Their website may look home-made but their Energysaver online tariff is worth considering (utilita.co.uk/prices.htm).

"Both paperless billing and online meter readings save your energy supplier a lot of money – savings that can then be passed on to you and also cut down the amount of wasted paper", reports Energy Choices. You can find out more about saving money by switching to online energy tariffs via energychoices.co.uk/online-energy-tariffs.html.

Compare Prices And Switch Supplier

With online price comparison websites for anything from airport parking to books, you won't be surprised to find a whole stack that monitor the prices of **gas**, **electricity** and other **home utilities** and dump them into a vast, searchable consumer database, all designed to help save us money (and make them a mint in the process). In 2002, **Energywatch** (now **Consumer Focus**) launched a voluntary code of practice for these websites. You can download a copy, if you so desire, from consumerfocus.org.uk/en/content/cms/Energy_Help___Advice/Helping_Households/Price_comparison_ser/Price_comparison_ser.aspx and see for yourself how the comparison sites are measured. But the end result of this is that it has so far accredited the following nine websites to the **Consumer Focus Confidence Code**.

Confused.com

Covered in detail in Chapter 14, **Confused.com** claims that – across 2008 – UK customers who used them to compare and switch gas and electricity (dual fuel) saved on average £252.37.

Chapter 15

Dual Fuel – Dual Saving

Are you on a **dual fuel tariff**? In other words, do you pay a single fee for both your gas and electricity? Most of the energy suppliers offer these, and a noticeable saving for combining your payments into one, as a way to gain customer loyalty. "Because of the discounts offered to tempt you to sign up, it's true that dual fuel tariffs are usually the cheapest option for many customers", reports Energy Choices. "The discounts offered on dual fuel tariffs do mean that they're often the best deal to be had. So if you're looking for the cheapest gas and electricity around, an online only, dual fuel tariff will undoubtedly be the one for you." Find out more from energychoices.co.uk/energy-tariff-options.html.

Energyhelpline.com

Worth checking for their **green energy** section, and info on home emergency and central heating insurance policies. They can also manage your energy supplier switch over the phone for you.

Energylinx

Energylinx (energylinx.co.uk) claims to be "the largest specialist domestic energy price comparison site in the UK", and has certainly provided its users with some impressive savings. When I checked in with them, in the previous sixty days (18 May 2009 to 16 July 2009), their customers had saved an average of £140.95 off their annual bills. But one user had gone way above average, raking in a saving of £1583!

Hidden Benefits

Many energy suppliers offer good rates, but few of them make them visible and easy to access (especially for existing customers). Such cheap tariffs "are only available if you actively seek them out", reports *The Guardian*'s Lisa Bachelor. "Energy companies won't usually tell you about them and you won't be put on an online tariff by asking over the phone. Existing British Gas customers, for example, will have to switch to the Click Energy 2 tariff online either via **Clickenergy.co.uk** or one of several price comparison websites." Find out more in *Take Back The Power: How To Beat The Utility Giants* at guardian.co.uk/money/2007/may/06/consumernews.utilities.

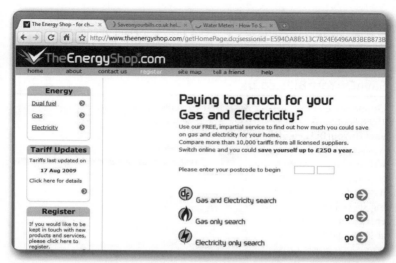

TheEnergyShop.com

The most basic of all, **TheEnergyShop.com** is the only site to tackle the one thing that many users have in the back of their mind – how do these sites actually make money? Have a read of their section entitled *How Can We Offer This Service For Free?* (theenergyshop.com/howWeOfferTESForFree.jsp) where they also point out that their "commercial relationships with all the main licensed domestic energy suppliers" also mean that "in certain cases we can offer you exclusive deals that are more competitive than you can get if you call the supplier directly."

HomeAdvisoryService.co.uk

This is another site that promises you won't find cheaper deals elsewhere. That's possibly because, unlike insurance comparison sites, for example, all the energy sites scan the same sources. What they lack in layout and information overload, they make up for with a wide range of personal finance advice.

Moneysupermarket.com

As covered in Chapter 14, this is the longest-running of the UK comparison sites, having launched in 1999. And this is the best of all sites for

Chapter 15

associated content; they also provide info on understanding your bills (moneysupermarket.com/c/gas-and-electricity/bills) and offer a regularly updated chart of which suppliers' prices are increasing, dropping or staying static. It's at moneysupermarket.com/utilities/gas-electricity-prices.aspx.

SaveOnYourBills.co.uk

Online since 1999, Scotland's **SaveOnYourBills.co.uk** was one of the first websites to gain **Ofgem** accreditation. They also have a newsletter covering special offers and new energy tariffs (subscribe at saveonyourbills.co.uk/domestic/newsletter_registration.jsp). "We do

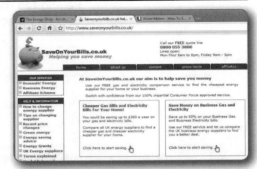

not send these out every week", they promise, "only when we have a really good offer for you to help you save money."

SimplySwitch (simplyswitch.com)

SimplySwitch (simplyswitch.com) have a dedicated telephone response service, a claim that they "won't be beaten on price", and regular updates on all the new tariffs. Many customers have made a £200 saving on annual fuel costs and you can read what they have to say at simplyswitch.com/testimonials-full.html.

UKPower.co.uk

Whether you use this site for your comparisons or not, it's still well worth checking out for its unique energy cost calculator, otherwise known as **MySmartMeter**. Go to smartmeter.ukpower.co.uk and have your meter readings and current supplier and tariff info to hand. Enter your details and MySmartMeter will then calculate how much gas or electricity you have used, what prices you can expect, your daily consumption and your carbon footprint.

Reasons To Be Switchful

If you're coming round to the idea of **utility switching** from cold, as it were, **Yahoo! Finance** sets out ten useful facts at uk.biz.yahoo.com/utilities/switching_with_yahoo.html, and **UtiliHub** lists its own interesting reasons at utilihub.com/why_change.html. But these are the reasons that do it for me:

1 It can save you money Obviously. That's why it's earned a chapter of this book in its own right.

2 It could save you a LOT of money uSwitch.com quotes up to £3251 per year.

3 It's free There are no fees for cutting off one supplier and starting up with another.

4 It's not the nightmare you might think You're only changing your billing company – not the one that installs or maintains your pipes or wires or electricity pylons.

5 Your supply won't be interrupted Rest assured that you won't be left with some scary changeover period when your lights go out for a few days.

6 It's easy An hour or two at your computer screen and a few letters and signatures by post should sort it.

Unravelit

Being the only site mentioned so far with a detailed and regularly updated blog makes **Unravelit** (unravelit.com) well worth a look. It covers the facts on fixed-price energy deals, the effects of the budget, tips on cutting energy consumption and more.

uSwitch.com

The most proactive site, **uSwitch.com** has video guides, including one on *How to Shrink Your Energy Bills* (uswitch.com/gas-electricity/how-to-shrink-your-energy-bills-video) and a campaign for simpler, clearer and easier bills based on a survey of their users.

Which? Switch

A spin-off from the long-running consumer advice association, **Which?** (switchwithwhich.co.uk) claims that average annual savings per household that switched via their service between 1 August 2008 and 13 December 2008 were an impressive £257.

> ## What About Water?
>
> You can't switch **water provider** like you can for gas and electricity, but UK readers can however be as cost efficient as possible by weighing up how to pay – either with a water meter or a trad water bill. The difference in expense can be considerable. The only comparison site tackling this issue is **uSwitch.com**. They have a detailed questionnaire that will help you find out if you're better off being metered and paying for your exact usage, or if you should be paying a standard bill based on an average estimate. It's all at uswitch.com/water/how-to-switch-water.
>
> For a US take on things, **The Frugal Life** offers an extensive list of tips on how to cut down your water bill, courtesy of Dr Charlotte Gorman. It's at thefrugallife.com/waterbill.html. **American Water** has a set of *Awesome Tips* for saving water indoors and outdoors at americanwater.com/49ways_savintips.htm.

Making The Switch ... In The US

Many US states are tied into a single gas or electricity supplier, so switching to save money – or to go green – just isn't an option. But a new process of **deregulation** is starting to change things, and afford residents of some US states choice. Fourteen states have been deregulated so far: **Connecticut, Florida, Georgia, Illinois, Indiana, Kentucky, Maryland, Massachusetts, Michigan, New Jersey, New York, Ohio, Pennsylvania** and **Texas**. **British Columbia** and **Ontario** in Canada have also been deregulated.

As a result, US public authorities are very much in education mode for their citizens. "Millions of Texans have exercized their right to pick their **Retail Electric Provider** (REP) and a plan that is right for them", explains the **Texas Electric Choice** education programme (powertochoose.com). "With a wide variety of electricity products and plans available in the marketplace, you may find a plan that provides you with significant savings or provide more certainty than your current plan. You may also want to consider switching to an electricity product that uses primarily renewable energy. Some REPs also have other value-added services like air conditioning maintenance, rewards programs, or other customer service benefits."

Although there are no pure web-based comparison services, **energy consultancies** such as **Options Energy Consulting** in Toledo, Ohio, will take your details and shop around for you. "We obtain your annual usage from your home or business, we then submit the information to the suppliers

we know will provide the best pricing options and service", they explain on **ChooseUtility.com**. "We put together a cost analysis of your previous utility expenses over the last twelve months, and show you the benefits of choosing one of the suggested energy marketers…"

Making The Switch … In The UK

Once you've found a better deal, how exactly do you go about switching suppliers for something as embedded into your house as gas or electricity? It's relatively simple. The first stage is to **apply to your new supplier** (the

---

Prepayment Meter Rip-Offs

Do you pay for your gas and/or electricity on a prepayment meter? According to **National Energy Action** (nea.org.uk), 5.8 million people in the UK do. And, according to the **National Housing Federation** (housing.org.uk, which represents 1200 not-for-profit housing associations), users of said meters have been over-charged across 2006, 2007 and 2008 to the tune of a whopping £46 million. To try and reclaim your possible overpayment, the NHF website has template letters for you to send both to your local MP and to your energy supplier. You can join other consumers taking action on their **Facebook** page at facebook.com/group.php?gid=18177484655.

Home Energy Check

The Energy Saving Trust is a non-profit organization fighting climate change on a personal, domestic level, as well as on the international, corporate front. They offer a "home energy check" which, once you've filled out an online questionnaire, provides you with a free, impartial report on how you can save energy bills at home and benefit the environment at the same time. Find it at energysavingtrust.org.uk/What-can-I-do-today.

---

comparison site you use should supply a link to do this). "At this stage you may need to have your existing meter identification numbers available", recommends **Switchwise.com**. Known as an **MPAN number** for electricity suppliers, and an **MPR number** for gas, you'll find these on your most recent bill. Your application will then trigger letters from both your new and existing suppliers. Having filled in their forms – and, most likely, been subjected to please-don't-leave-us phone calls from your current supplier – they'll take care of the rest.

You'll probably be asked for **meter readings**, so your old supplier knows how much to charge for their final bill, and so your new one can start measuring how much gas or electricity you've used. For more, check the simple step-by-step guide at switchwise.com/energy/howtoswitch.

Usage Monitors

AlertMe takes Tescocompare.com's ideas on holiday unplugging (see box on p.142) one stage further. It's a new system that provides live updates and

---

Grant Eligible?

If you're over sixty, have a child under sixteen (or are pregnant), or if you are claiming benefit, then you might qualify for a government grant to make your home more energy efficient. The **Warm Front** scheme is a government-funded initiative which grants up to £3500 for insulation and heating improvements. Find out more at warmfront.co.uk. If you're in Wales, there's a similar scheme called the **Home Energy Efficiency** scheme, funded by the Welsh Assembly. They're at heeswales.co.uk.

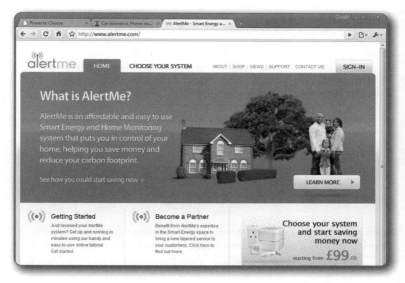

advice on your home energy consumption, by placing monitors on all plugs and switches which relay information back to your PC screen. Possibly easier to describe with pictures rather than words, you can see a graphical demo at alertme.com. A lot of people are getting very excited about AlertMe and systems like it, even though they're at quite an early stage in their development. Being able to monitor and control your energy usage "live" is a breakthrough – especially compared to the current situation where usage is estimated and

Fixed Rate – Time's Up?

A **fixed-price energy plan** is much the same as a fixed-price mortgage: you enjoy a flat monthly fee for a year while the market rate goes up, down, and up again. They were especially popular in the UK in 2008, when market prices started to rise. Normally set up across a **twelve-month contract**, you get very little warning when they expire and you flip straight on to the standard rate. This might mean a sudden price hike of around £100. So, if you're on a fixed-rate deal, make sure you **A) know when it's set to end and B) start your research on the comparison sites early**, as making a switch can take well over a month to come into effect.

Chapter 15

then billed for every month. As well as impacting your electricity bill, it might also make a significant environmental impact.

"Home energy usage accounts for more than one quarter of total energy consumption across Europe and the United States", AlertMe explains, "and consumers are increasingly looking for ways to save money and help the planet. Home energy-saving is the fastest and lowest-cost way to close the large gap between today's demand and what renewables can supply..."

Smart Meters

In spring 2009, the UK government pledged to roll out a far more basic, but still money-saving, version of AlertMe: **Smart Meters**. They'll be deployed in all homes over the next decade and you can find out more at energy-retail.org.uk/TheSmartMetersCampaign.html. Most importantly, **uSwitch.com** has already started to do the maths on what they will mean to your monthly outgoings. "Smart Meters will provide consumers with the information they need to manage their use of energy and reduce costs", said **uSwitch.com**'s Tom Lyon on the day the government announced the initiative. "At last, it will also mark the end of meter readings and estimated bills."

Avoiding Overpayment

With Smart Meters and AlertMe-style "total control" products some years off, we're stuck with paying for our household energy consumption based on monthly direct debits, signed up to in twelve-month stretches, based on estimates of consumption. So, even if you're good and unplug when you can, will you actually see your bill go down? Or are you more likely to have to continue overpaying, building up more and more credit on your account (which, when replicated across hundreds of thousands of consumers, becomes a tidy sum for the energy companies to sit on and earn interest off)?

"If a customer is in credit, it needs to be made crystal-clear on the bill, with a telephone number clearly visible so a customer can claim their cash back", **Energywatch**'s (now known as **Consumer Focus**, consumerfocus.org .uk) Adam Scorer told the press when *Which?* magazine first flagged this issue. And, as **uSwitch.com** added, "Not everyone will automatically send you a refund cheque, but most will on request or will modify your payments automatically. Our advice is that, if you are paying by direct debit, check on a quarterly basis exactly how much you're using with a proper reading – most companies will listen if you challenge them, making a correction on a 12-monthly basis."

Another reason to stay on top of your payments – or overpayments – comes from *The Guardian*'s Adrian Holliday who pointed out that, "Worryingly, if a utility firm collapses with money still owed to you, getting it back is not guaranteed. Ofgem, the regulator for gas and electricity markets, says customers would need to join the queue for the administrators if a utility firm hit the buffers – so a dismal chance of getting near the top of the creditor list." You can read his full coverage of this potential money-saving issue at guardian.co.uk/money/2003/jan/05/utilities.observerbusiness, along with top tips on managing your utility bills. As he says, "If you're £50 in credit, why not claim it back and earn some interest on it?"

16

Travel For Less

Have A Break ... Save Some Cash

From British Airways to Hilton Hotels, the big travel companies pay a fortune for their adverts to appear prominently when you use Google to search for holiday destinations and to plan your vacation. But there are lots of websites that will get you from A to B far cheaper, and which will help you plan a memorable holiday no matter what the state of your finances.

The most popular travel and accommodation websites – **Expedia**, **Travelocity** and the like – can all save you money and help you comparison shop. So, stage one: **start planning your vacation online** using one of these to build an itinerary, get some ideas for where you could go, and to get an idea of prices for flights, transport and accommodation. Then comes stage two: **browse the rest of the sites in this chapter** to find alternative, cheaper options for each stage of your journey.

And stage three? Always **check the websites of the hotel or airline you choose** to make sure they don't offer special deals for travellers buying direct.

Package Holidays Post-Teletext

For years, the TV-based **Teletext** system was the place to look "online" in the UK for late deals and good prices for buying a package holiday in Europe. Initially set to close in 2011, the recession brought Teletext's deadline forward to January 2010 when it will go off air for good. So where can you go online for your package holiday bargains?

Holiday Discount Centre (holidaydiscountcentre.co.uk) is a good answer to that question. It covers all the major package operators: **Cosmos**, **First Choice**, **Thomson** and the like. And it boasts a healthy set of customer service awards. **Directline Holidays** (directline-holidays.co.uk) and **Package Holidays** (2009packageholidays.co.uk) are both also worth considering.

The US equivalent of these are **discount tour operators** who provide special deals on combined hotel/air packages. Three to try are **TourCrafters** (tourcrafters.com), **Vacation Outlet** (vacationoutlet.com), and **Vacation Express** (vacationexpress.com).

As travel expert and blogger Christopher Elliot (elliott.org) points out, "nearly every hotel chain now offers a lowest-rate guarantee for guests who book online through their site directly." He also recommends weighing up booking direct in case you've chosen one of the many hotels that "will even offer a free night if you find one of their rooms for less on another site." His **Online Travel, Version 2.0** blog at elliott.org/the-travel-technologist/online-travel-version-20 is always well worth a read.

Here's a look at the main players worth checking out, before you check in...

Expedia

The biggest online travel agent, **Expedia** (expedia.com) covers everything from hotels to flights to package holidays. And their range of choice is staggering: four million rooms across eighty thousand hotels, motels and Holiday Inns, airfares available to book from any one of 450 airlines, booking systems linked into all the main car hire companies, timetables, weather info, and so on. There's no wonder it consistently ranks as one of the top one thousand websites in the world, and that more than ten thousand websites link to it. You could say it's the Microsoft of travel websites … which would be right, because it was started by Microsoft, and then spun off into a separate company when its success started to spiral skywards.

Chapter 16

So can you find bargains on such a monstrously monopolizing site as this? Definitely. Like eBay it thrives by giving small players (in this case thousands of hotels and hotel chains) a platform to be shopped from, compared on price and joined up to make a best-value travel itinerary.

You can find late availability bargains on **flights** by going direct to expedia.co.uk/daily/stores/flights/flightdeals.aspx. Of, if you're looking for a bargain **hotel**, remember that all of their latest cheap hotel prices always go live on the site on Fridays. So make a date in the diary to check the site then, and get in before anyone else. If you're laying in wait to find a good deal on a flight to a particular airport, download Expedia's **Fare Alert software**. You enter the flight you're after and the fare you'd like to pay and, when it finds a deal that matches (or beats) it, an alert will pop up on screen ready for you to click through and purchase. This is only available to US users, via expedia.com/daily/highlights/fare_alert/default.asp.

The other way to get some money off your Expedia travel itinerary

Crafty Passports

If you're applying for – or renewing – your **UK passport**, then the **Home Office Identity & Passport Service** website (ips.gov.uk) is full of useful information. But here's how to save a substantial sum – and subvert one of their money-making policies – when you have a question. The most common questions, of course, are "where is my new passport?", "when will I receive it?" and "will I receive it before my day of travel?" This was exactly what I wanted to know while writing this book, so I emailed the Home Office. Instead of getting an email reply with the answer, I received three things. A voicemail message asking me to phone them to check the status, a text message to my mobile with the same response, and an email with – you guessed it – the same response. Three attempts to have me call a number that's charged at £1.50 per minute. The alternative? I checked for "passport" and "Home Office" enquiry numbers on **Saynoto0870 .com**, found one that looked like it fitted the bill and called. I got straight through and, three minutes later, had spoken to a very helpful member of staff who answered all my questions. Total cost: nothing. Total cost if I'd have followed the advice in their email, voicemail and text: at least £4.50.

One last thing on passports: in the US, you can avoid waiting in line to renew your passport by going to travel.state.gov/passport/get/renew/renew_833.html where you'll find step-by-step instructions and all the necessary forms to download.

is to **Google for coupons and vouchers**. The web is awash with different sites collating and offering discount vouchers for Expedia so do one of two things. Either narrow your search for the exact destination and dates you're after. Or go to a reputable source of discount codes and vouchers; try either couponing.about.com or frugalsavers.com. You'll find more on online discounts, vouchers and coupons in Chapter 19.

Trip Advisor & Travelocity

Trip Advisor (tripadvisor.com) and **Travelocity** (travelocity.com) both offer a similar comparison-style service to Expedia and are worth testing out. Trip Advisor thrives on user reviews, forums and photos which is especially useful when you're planning a trip to somewhere you've never been. They have nine thousand free travel guides available to download, covering destinations from Dublin to Dubai at tripadvisor.com/TravelGuides. And they have dedicated sister sites covering **cheap flights** (bookingbuddy.com) and another for comparing airplane seating, in-flight amenities and **airline information** at seatguru.com.

Chapter 16

Over on Travelocity, head straight to travelocity.com/Travel-Deals and travelocity.com/sale where they have a regularly updated set of credit crunch-friendly offers. Here, you'll find their *100 Under $100* list covering US hotels available to book for under $100 per night.

Orbitz & Priceline.Com

While it's worth checking hotel and flight sites direct, just to make sure you've got the best deal possible from Expedia or one of its competitors, **Orbitz** (orbitz.com) attempts to sidestep this and retain customers by offering an aggressive price-matching policy. "Here's how it works", they explained when their **Hotel Price Assurance** service launched in May 2009. "You book any pre-paid hotel on Orbitz, another Orbitz customer subsequently books the same hotel stay at a lower rate, and Orbitz automatically sends you a cheque for the difference."

Despite being US-centric, Orbitz is possibly the best online travelplex for good deals and discounts. They also have a similar price assurance policy for flight bookings, and don't charge any booking fees for flights. There are sections dedicated to **last-minute travel deals**, **round-trip fares** under $200 and so on. **Priceline.com** offers something similar, including an offer to "eliminate all Priceline cancellation and change fees on every published-price airline ticket, hotel room, rental car, cruise and vacation package where changes or cancellations are allowed."

Holiday Money: Cash Vs Plastic

Price-conscious holidaymakers are more and more choosing to take cash abroad with them. The reason? Well, despite security factors, it can cost a small fortune to spend money on plastic abroad, whether by credit card or at an ATM.

For example, according to **No1 Currency**, British holidaymakers squandered an eye-watering "£784 million on credit and debit card charges last year." So, who gives the best deal for foreign currency? No1 thinks they do and have a chart pitting themselves against other major outlets at no1currency.com/bureau-de-change/rates.asp.

But there are alternatives, such as **TravelMoneyMax.com,** the spin-off site from the UK's online money-saving bible, **MoneySavingExpert.com**. Whereas **No1 Currency** charts its value for money against a handful of other forex outlets, TravelMoneyMax.com surveys twenty outlets and is full of info and advice on getting the most from your holiday spending money.

For example, "don't change cash at the airport", they advised on launch. "The first ever true holiday cash comparison site, TravelMoneyMax.com, definitively proves those who wait to change money at airports are wasting a fortune. On £500, you'd be fifty dollars and forty euros worse off, and, while High Street forex bastions **Marks & Spencer** and the **Post Office** are better, even they're blown away by the top providers."

Kayak

With so many online travel agencies to check out, this might all get a bit confusing, and a bit of a chore. But then along comes **Kayak** (kayak.com), a simple, Google-like website that searches all the travel sites for you. "Kayak was started by founders of Orbitz, Travelocity and Expedia", they explain, "who believed in a better online travel experience. They hired a crack team of geeky engineers who brought expertise from all over the Web and redefined the way people search and purchase travel online."

They also have tips on finding "the LFP (lowest fare possible)", an **iPhone app** (blog.kayak.com/2009/05/19/kayak-iphone-app-updated) and the coolest "meet the team" page of any website in this book, or possibly any business website around (kayak.co.uk/team). But if you struggle with Kayak, try its Edinburgh-based rival, **Skyscanner** (skyscanner.net).

Chapter 16

RoadTripHelper.com

For a map-based, hotel-specific version of Kayak, check out **RoadTripHelper .com**. This is a great site for finding the best price on a city-based hotel, especially if you want to stay close to a particular landmark, museum or attraction. It claims to be "the world's largest online hotel database", because it simultaneously searches **Hotels.com**, **Expedia**, **Travelocity**, **Orbitz** and various others. You can then narrow your search based on a specific map location, pinpointed on an embedded map from **Google Maps**. A neat trick, and a friendly site.

SimonSeeks Sets Sail

If you're a traveller that likes to write, the new website from Simon Nixon, founder of **Moneysupermarket.com**, might make you a little money or – at the very least – help steer you to the best destinations. "With **SimonSeeks** (simonseeks.com), he wants to try to replicate the usability of websites that he admires, such as **YouTube** and **Twitter** (on which he regularly tweets)", explained *The Times* when the site launched in July 2009, "and allow visitors to search for tailored travel guides ... Contributors of well-read reviews can expect to earn as much as £200 to £500 a year." You'd earn this when someone read your review and clicked through to an online travel agent to make a booking, at which point the fee the agent pays SimonSeeks is split 50/50 with the writer. Find out more at business.timesonline.co.uk/tol/business/industry_sectors/leisure/article6719630.ece.

Travelzoo & Lastminute.com

All of the travel sites in this chapter push their email newsletters as a way to tempt you to part with personal data in return for the latest breaking deals. Many are mere marketing ploys but the one e-zine that's really worth signing up to is from **Travelzoo** (travelzoo.com). As *The Daily Telegraph* says, this site is "famed for its Top 20 of the best offers on the Internet" and these are hand-picked and published every Wednesday in their e-mail newsletter, the most popular travel newsletter on the Internet. Another newsletter that's worth signing up for, if you're in the US, comes from **SmartTravel** (smartertravel .com). As Susan Breslow Sardone, **About.com**'s travel expert explains, "I prefer the **Smarter Living email newsletters** because they look at all the airlines and then send a customized report informing me of the latest travel bargains departing from my local airport."

Chapter 16

Travel Articles & Tips

All UK newspapers cover travel, of course, and they all occasionally cover budget travel. But only *The Daily Telegraph* has a full online section devoted to the subject, with articles on everything from *Jamaican Riches* At A Nice Price to *50 Of The Best Long-Haul Deals*. It's at telegraph.co.uk/travel/budgettravel. For more discursive, US-centric reading, try **Lifehacker** which has a section dedicated to summer activities and articles ranging from *Make Frozen Yogurt Pops for a Unique Summer Dessert* to *DIY Combination Sunscreen and Bug Repellent*. It's at lifehacker.com/tag/summer.

Back on Travelzoo, you can also find the latest bargain flights and hotels in their **Top 20 Deals** and **Last-Minute Travel** pages which, in the UK, are at uk.top20.travelzoo.com and uk.last-minute.travelzoo.com respectively. Talking of last-minute bookings, the website that everyone's heard of is **Lastminute .com**. One of the original online travel agencies, today they are of interest for the experiments going on at labs.lastminute.com. Here they are developing a raft of very nifty **Internet- and iPhone-based apps** for finding hotels and

Links & Tip-Offs

Here's a quick run-through of more than a dozen further websites that will help you plan a recession-friendly holiday or awayday. If you're in the US and planning a budget trip to Europe, check **EuroCheapo** (eurocheapo.com) and **Guideforeurope.com**. If you'd like a cruise, the best sites for discounts and comparisons are **iCruise.com** and **eCruises.com**. **Cruise Compete** (cruisecompete .com) works slightly differently: you set out where you'd like to go and how, and various cruise agencies provide quotes to take you there. If you plan to hitch-hike or just want to swap or share lifts to work, try **Carshare.com** and **Car-Pool .co.uk**. There is no shortage of travel forums where you can ask about, and find out about, cheap deals and the Facebook-style **WAYN** (wayn.com) is a great place to start. Sitting somewhere between a house-swap and a hotel is a hostel. Between them, **Hostelbookers.com** and **Hostelworld.com** have them covered. If you're going for hostels, you're probably backpacking. If so, check **Backpackers .com**, **Backpacker.net** and **Backpack Europe on a Budget** (backpackeurope.com) where you'll find plenty of money-saving advice. But the ones to try first are the ones with the best names: **TravelPUNK.com** and the **Travelbum Network** (travelbum.net).

Feeling Sleepy?

The website that really takes the cake for offering travellers advice on getting something for nothing has to be **Sleepinginairports.net**. "Why spend money on a night in the airport hotel when an inflatable raft on the airport floor is free?" the home page proclaims! "Sure, it may sound a little cheap and degrading at first, but read on and you'll soon discover a travel community, that for 13 years has been sharing their airport sleeping experiences and travel advice with fellow airport sleepers around the world."

---

holiday facilities. Also with Lastminute.com you can book a hotel room up until 10pm on the night of your stay, and get up to 45 percent off some of them by using their mysterious **Top Secret Hotels** service (lastminute.com/site/travel/hotels/deals/top-secret.html). "We bring you up to an additional 45 percent off our already discounted rates", they explain. "In order for us to bring you these exclusive deals, we are not allowed to tell you the name of the hotel, until you've completed your booking!"

TripPlanner & Trip Watcher

If you're **holidaying on a budget**, chances are you'll be flexible about when you travel and the particular route you take to your destination. With this in mind, **Hotwire** (hotwire.com) has a special booking system called **Trip Watcher** (hotwire.com/trip-watcher/index.jsp). "Trip Watcher considers your dates, destination, and (if flying) possible airports", they explain, "and compares them with Hotwire itineraries. If there's a way for you to get there for less – moving your trip a day, or using another airport – we'll let you know." Another way you can use Trip Watcher is to tell them where you would like to go and when – within a sixty-day period – and their site will watch all of those dates at once and come back with the lowest-priced travel days.

The other useful tool worth checking out on Hotwire is called **TripPlanner** (hotwire.com/tripstarter/index.jsp). You type in your favourite destination and it recommends the best time of year to visit, based on price, weather, local events, attractions, and so on.

Cheap & Cheapo

For US readers, two other mass-market travel agency sites are worth checking for discounted airline tickets. **CheapTickets** (cheaptickets.com) and **CheapOair**

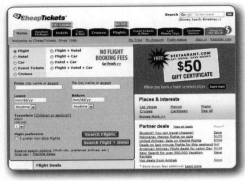

(cheapoair.com). The former has the biggest variety of travel options (and is one of the few travel agency websites mentioned so far to even *acknowledge* that **rail travel** exists). And the latter has the best selection of deals and discounts, such as flights under $199 and four-star hotels under $99 per night.

Staycations

In any recession, travel and holiday plans often focus closer to home. Why spend money travelling abroad when you could spend next to nothing exploring the countryside around you? The idea of holidaying at home (or, as *The Guardian* newspaper calls it, a "staycation"), is great … but where to go, and what can you expect when you get there? To fill a map with geo-tagged photos of staycation destinations, *The Guardian* created a **Flickr** group at flickr.com/groups/staycation09 which might just give you some ideas of where to go if your international travel plans are on ice. And you can read more about the idea at guardian.co.uk/travel/2009/may/18/staycation-flickr-group-photography-geo.

Can They Be Trusted?

There's one big difference between booking into a hotel and using a site like **CrashPadder.com** or **UKHolidaySwapShop.co.uk**, which is the issue of trust. You're buying from people rather than businesses so, just like the eBay world, you need to be ultra-careful and ultra-choosy. CrashPadder.com has an eBay-style **feedback system**, so you can read what other travellers have had to say about your prospective landlords. As founder Steven Rapoport told *The Times* (property.timesonline.co.uk/tol/life_and_style/property/article5244784.ece), "I believe that most people are basically good. There's always a risk with strangers, but you just have to use your head – and the security measures on the site."

UKHolidaySwapShop.co.uk

You may have used the Internet to get the best price for your vacation accommodation, but you could use it to get it completely free. Enter **UKHolidaySwapShop.co.uk**, which launched in 2009 and – inspired by the likes of **Home Link International** (homelink.org) and **Home Base Holidays** (homebase-hols.com) – is a directory of homes available for swap across the UK and Northern Ireland. Neither party involved in the swap exchanges any money, only their homes – and their trust – for the period of their stay. The only monetary cost is the £14 fee to list your house on the website.

Bargain Booze Cruise

Here's how to get away from it all and enjoy some cheap French wine at the same time. Check **Day-tripper.net** for some great last-minute and discount ferry trips to France. Cross-reference with **Ferrysavers.co.uk** and **FerryCheap.com** to make sure you're getting the best deal. Then head off and do what all Brits do best: hoover up the cheap wine, mustard and cheese. But make sure you know a bargain when you see it. Sites like **Tesco Vin Plus** (tesco-france.com) will help you make a comparison with the prices available at home.

Chapter 16

CrashPadder.com

But what about international travels, singles or couples and year-out types? For you, the best website is **CrashPadder.com**. As the team behind the site says, "CrashPadder.com is a glorious, Utopian ideal borne out of a simple desire to travel around, without having to pay a king's ransom for a place to lay your head." Unlike **UKHolidaySwapShop.co.uk** it's free to join and register your spare room, front room or sofa bed on the site. You can then choose how much you want to charge for it, the site handles payment and takes ten percent. So for those with space to let it's an easy way to make a little money,

and meet new people. And for travellers and backpackers it's a great source of discount accommodation. If you can't find a crashpad to your taste, try **The Hospitality Club** (hospitalityclub.org) and **CouchSurfing** (couchsurfing .org) which both provide a similar service.

17

Calling & Connecting

Software And Computing, Windows-Free And Licence-Free

As most computer geeks will tell you, it's possible to fully kit out your computer for nothing. No need to pay Microsoft for Word, Internet Explorer or even Windows. There are other, equally reliable, feature-rich (and often faster) alternatives out there. For anything software-related, your first port of call should be Download.com (download

.cnet.com), a virtual megastore of software for just about everything, where every application comes with a free trial version (if it's not free to use altogether).

With thousands of free applications on **Download.com**, and millions more around the net, it would be crazy to cover them all here. So let's keep it simple, and look at the ten low-cost and no-cost alternatives to paid-for software. And if you get your actual hardware via **Freecycle.org** (see p.93), then you could go from the stone age to being online by paying nothing more than … well … the price of this book.

Software Essentials

Free Operating Systems

Assume for a moment we're doing this from scratch. You've spent some of your hard-earned cash on a laptop – or maybe you've picked one up for nothing – and you want to get yourself up and running. The first thing you need to do is wipe off Windows. Microsoft is very hot on licence fees and that's a cost you can save. **Ubuntu** is an operating system which is free, and fast. You

Free Photoshopping

As **ReadWriteWeb**'s blogger Jolie O'Dell points out, "Photoshop, Adobe's industry standard for image editing, costs a whopping, unforgivable $600." She provides a brilliant set of completely free alternatives in *Free Alternatives to Photoshop With All the Bells, Whistles, Filters, & Layers* at readwriteweb.com/archives/free_alternatives_to_photoshop_with_all_the_bells.php, **including** ReadWriteWeb readers' favourite **Paint.NET** (getpaint.net), open-souce desktop app **The GIMP** (gimp.org) and the sexily interfaced **Splashup** (splashup.com).

don't have the support of a multinational company behind you, but you do have the support of its millions of users. You can download Ubuntu for free from ubuntu.com/getubuntu or if you can't get online yet go to an Internet café and request a free CD version from shipit.ubuntu.com.

Taking its name from an African phrase meaning "humanity to others", there are special versions of Ubuntu available for desktop, laptop and netbook computers (as well as schools, servers, and all sorts). And it comes with a suite of free Windows-like **apps**: **word processing**, **email** and so on.

Another possibility is the **Google Chrome** operating system. At the time of writing it has not yet been released, but should be available for download from Google by the time you read this. It is expected to be fast, lightweight, specifically tailored for use with Web-based tools, and best of all, free.

Word Processing And Office Tools

New PCs often come pre-installed with a trial of **Microsoft Office**. You then have to deal with the tiresome pop-up warning after the trial period has expired, asking you for money. If you're a **Word**, **Excel**, or **PowerPoint** user, you'll find similar applications bundled free with Ubuntu. There's more info on each here: ubuntu.com/products/whatisubuntu/904features/office-tools/.

Chapter 17

More Open-Source Software

The open-source developer community, which gave the world **OpenOffice**, is a thriving hotbed of cost-free alternatives to all sorts of other software. A good directory site, which allows you to search for apps by the name of their costly alternatives, is **Osalt.com**, aka **Open Source as ALTernative**.

For a more fully functioning alternative to Microsoft Office, consider OpenOffice. This software suite has been around since the late 1990s, when it was known as **StarOffice**, a product from Sun Microsystems. Since then it's been taken over by the open source community, **OpenOffice.org**, and grown organically into a completely viable alternative to **Microsoft Office**. Head to openoffice.org/product/ to find out more and to download.

Although OpenOffice can do pretty much everything Microsoft Office can, hardened Windows users will still feel a little like fish out of water. All the buttons and options are there: you just need to get used to looking in a slightly different place! So if you're bashing your head against a brick wall, check this handy comparison chart at documentation.openoffice.org/HOW_TO/word_processing/Word-to-OOo.html.

The other completely free alternative to Microsoft Office is **Google Docs**. Unlike OpenOffice, this one takes quite a leap of imagination if you're used to the standard Microsoft way of doing things. And it's **completely web-based**, which might not suit you if you like to work at the bottom of the garden, or if you don't have a consistent, reliable Internet connection. But the big benefit of online tools like this is collaboration. If you're working on a spreadsheet, you can set it up so other people can view it or make amends.

Take a guided tour of Google Docs at google.com/google-d-s/tour1.html.

Free Broadband

Is it possible to get online for nothing? A host of "free broadband" deals from ISPs and telecom companies are out there to tempt you. And many mobile and cable TV networks offer attractive broadband packages for existing customers. **Broadband Choices** has a YouTube video explaining more at youtube.com/watch?v=E9qv67glH7o, and there's a roundup of twenty different free suppliers at the comparison site **Top 10 Broadband** (top10-broadband.co.uk/compare/free_broadband).

Calling & Connecting

Free Wi-Fi

Say you've got yourself a laptop for nothing from Freecycle, installed a free operating system and a free browser. You can now trot off to anywhere from a hotel
to a library and take advantage of their **free wireless Internet**. The **Wi-Fi-FreeSpot
Directory** (wififreespot.com) provides state-by-state listings of free Wi-Fi available in the US and at various locations around Europe. And **Airportwifiguide.com**
details the availability of free Wi-Fi around the world's airports.

Or try the far simpler and easy to understand *Google Docs in Plain English*
video at youtube.com/watch?v=eRqUE6IHTEA.

Explorer Alternatives

Millions of Internet users browse the Web using Microsoft's paid-for web
browser, **Internet Explorer** (IE), by default. You probably use it just because
it comes pre-loaded. But not only could you avoid paying licence fees by
removing it (or buying a PC without it), you could also speed up your browsing experience.

Google launched its own, free web browser in 2008. It's called **Chrome**
(like their operating system, see p.159) and is different to IE in two main

ways: it's faster, and far simpler to configure. It's also built, unsurprisingly, with ease-of-search in mind, and has a handy "incognito window" function for private browsing. All is explained at google.co.uk/chrome.

Chrome isn't the most popular IE alternative, though. That prize is taken by Mozilla's **Firefox**. You can download a copy, and watch a video review of the myriad features at download.cnet.com/mozilla-firefox.

Virus Protection

Outside of working and browsing, the other main use of a computer is communicating – an activity well served by free software and services. Free email (**Hotmail**, **Yahoo! Mail**, **Google Mail**, and so on) and instant messaging services (**MSN Messenger** and the like) are not hard to track down.

But the more you browse, email and collaborate online, the more you open yourself up to **virus attacks**. And there's a whole industry out there hyping the latest viruses, and scaremongering about phishing and trojans, in the hope that we'll all run petrified to them and offload some cash on the latest anti-virus (AV) or security software suite. Whilst all the name-brand AV vendors certainly offer a lot of features, this is not something you really need to pay for. **PC Tools**, **Avasti** and **AVG** are all tried-and-tested makers of reliable, credible and free anti-virus software:

- **Avasti** avast.com/eng/avast_4_home.html
- **AVG** free.avg.com/download
- **PC Tools** pctools.com/free-antivirus

Calling Out Around The World

From subverting corporate enquiry lines to computer-based phone calls, here are seven ways to save money on your mobile and landline calls:

1 Get cash for your old handset mobile There's a raft of Internet sites out there with one simple message and, to quote the site that shouts loudest, **Envirofone.com**, "get cash for your old mobile phones!" They estimate that there are more than eighty million unwanted handsets swishing around the UK, with a total recyclable value of £1.6 billion. They're desperate to collect your old handset (even paying a courier if you have four or more to dispose of) and will pay you a fee for each one. In fact, since they started out, the

company has paid out £20 million for old phones, recycling them all and donating £500,000 to charity in the process. Also try **Mazuma** (mazumamobile .com), **Mopay .co.uk** (who provide shopping vouchers as opposed to cash), or **Mobile Cash Comparison** (mobile-cash-comparison .co.uk). In the US, go straight to **Cellforcash.com** to get a price.

2 Compare handsets and operators Right Mobile Phone (rightmobilephone .co.uk) is a good place to start, asking you for everything from your preferred handset brand to preferred number of free monthly texts, before coming back with its recommendations. You can also search with a real money-saving attitude, checking out

only the contracts that provide cashback, for example, or – more enjoyable still – browse their parade of free gifts currently available from operators (everything from laptops and PSPs to TVs are up for grabs). A simple Google search will yield plenty of options for more cellphone comparison sites. But the one that takes the cake for coolness, and for making comparing deals actually quite good fun, is **Omio** (omio.com). In the US try **Wirefly.com** and **Letstalk.com**.

3 ...or choose a discount handset Operating outside of the High Street, and with only low-grade websites to show off their wares, are a set of discount

Chapter 17

phone and airtime websites which can get you kitted out with a mobile and contract for much less than you might expect. The main ones to try are **Dial-a-Phone** (dialaphone.co.uk), the Car Phone Warehouse's **One Stop Phone Shop** (onestopphoneshop.co.uk) and **MobileShop.com**.

4 Avoid premium rate phone lines The most horribly designed site in this whole book is also the one which could save you a decent amount of money on a daily basis. The UK is awash with businesses – and public services – using paid phone lines for customer enquiries. The way to avoid losing money if you need to dial a business or public service with a number beginning with

0500, 0800, 0808, 0844, 0845, 0870 or 0871 (which could cost you up to 15p per minute) is to check for a national call-rate alternative number on **Saynoto0870.com**. While there, you can also sign their petition against the NHS's use of 0844 and 0845 numbers by clicking over to petitions.number10. gov.uk/Healthtelephone.

5 Use free alternatives to directory enquiries You can run up quite a phone bill by calling the three main directory enquiries lines in the UK. **BT** (118 500), **Conduit** (118 888) and **The Number** (118 118) are the main operators, and they're not cheap. A call to 118 500, for example, costs 40p to connect plus 99p per minute for the duration of the call. If you go online, however, you can find all the numbers you need for nothing. **192.com** is the best, and has five gongs from the **118 Awards** to prove it. If you think you're going to need a directory enquiries service while you're on the move – and away from an Internet signal – have a quick read of **Free Directory Enquiries Ltd**'s website (freedirectoryenquiries.com) before you set off. They don't have a web-based enquiry engine, but their site will furnish you with details of their completely free phone-based system. In short, you call 0800 100 100, ask their operator for your desired number, which they'll give you after playing a short advert. Or, if you call from a mobile, they'll text you back with the number alongside a text-based advert. In the US, try Google's free directory service: 1-800-GOOG-411.

6 Don't pay through the nose to roam
Calling from abroad on your mobile used to be an incredibly expensive business. But this started to change when the EU set up some new rules for telecoms operators which came into effect in July 2009. You can get all the details on their specially created website at ec.europa.eu/roaming. This may sound like great news...
"But watch out if you are travelling **outside the EU**", says **Moneymagpie**'s Jasmine Birtles. In the supremely detailed *Cheaper Call Costs When You're Abroad* (moneymagpie.com/article/898/curb-call-costs-when-youre-abroad) she reports that "in order for network providers to compensate for having to reduce EU charges they have collectively increased their roaming charges outside the EU by 115%."

7 Avoid call costs altogether
In short, take your calls online using a **VOIP** (voice over IP) service. They offer very cheap rates for calls to regular numbers worldwide, and if you call other VOIP users on the same service, it's free. The most popular VOIP service is **Skype** (skype. com), a start-up which was acquired by eBay in August 2005. Having started in Luxembourg in 2002, by the time Skype partnered with eBay, the company had gathered 54 million users across 225 countries and was a household name in the propellerhead community. You can find out more with some introductions to VOIP from **What's A Byte?** (whatsabyte.com/P1/voip101.htm) and **Broadband.co.uk** (broadband.co.uk/guides/voip).

More Flavours Of VOIP

Before installing Skype, check out these four alternatives:

- **X-Lite 3** counterpath.com
- **Vbuzzer Messenger** vbuzzer.com
- **MagicBlock** vvisoft.com
- **iCall** icall.com

165

18

House Hunting

...And Home-Making

From avoiding estate agents' fees to finding house prices with fifty percent discounts, here's a step-by-step walk through the moving house scenario, checking off all the websites out there to save you money (and time) in the process.

Setting Your Price

The first thing you do when putting your house on the market is to check local prices and recent sales, to see what you might get (and to figure out if you agree with the sale price your estate agent proposes). So try **Nethouseprices** (nethouseprices.com), which is a free website that holds the final sales prices of all houses in England and Wales, dating back to January 1999 (and in Scotland going back to May 2000). You can search by postcode, street name or town.

House Hunting

When it comes to looking for a new house, you can save a lot of time, energy and money going from one estate agent window to another by searching one of the three main (UK) house hunting portals. **Rightmove.co.uk** claims to be the number one choice, while **Primelocation.com** represents more than two hundred independent estate agents. **Zoopla** (zoopla.co.uk), meanwhile, is a property website from the team behind online DVD rental giants **LOVEFiLM**. It has a unique feature which allows you to express your interest in any property, whether it's on the market or not. Log your preferences on their **TemptMe!** pages, and you'll get an alert when your preferred property comes on the market (and the current owners get to see how in-demand their house is). For the US market **Trulia.com** is a good bet.

Zoopla also includes embedded **Google Street View** functionality. So if there's a house you're interested in you can immediately see what the view is from the front door, and what kind of condition the neighbours' houses are in. If you're on a property site that doesn't offer Street View, just go off to maps.google.com/help/maps/streetview and type in the postcode to get started.

Chapter 18

I Am Moving.com

There are a couple of free services at **Iammoving.com** which will save you some time (and money) when moving day comes. Their **Change of Address** (CoA) service is well worth taking advantage of. You register and provide your old and new address details and they'll take care of informing more than 1500 organizations that might need to know, such as your utility suppliers, the DVLA, TV licence office and so on. While you're on their site, take a couple of clicks to work through their Data Protection Act database and put a stop to organizations sending you junk mail.

Know Your Neighbourhood

When you've found your dream home, you'll want to check out the area, the schools, and what the neighbourhood has to offer. The classic website for this is **UpMyStreet** (upmystreet.com). A simple postcode search will bring back information on crime rates, school league tables, prospective council tax payments, amenities and so on.

UpMyStreet is also great for background reading on all aspects of moving. Check upmystreet.com/home-finance/articles.html for items ranging from mortgage application tips to a chart of the worst places to live in the UK. **Homecheck** (homecheck.co.uk) offers similar neighbourhood statistics but adds some all-important environmental assessments, such as the likelihood of floods. On the downside, though, it offers very little information free of charge.

Once you've moved in, you might start to spot nagging local problems, like graffiti or litter. A great website to have on hand is **FixMyStreet** (fixmystreet.com). This one saves you time, money and gray hairs, and gives your local council an automated kick up the Internet at the same time. You just type in the street name where the problem is, the details of what's winding you up, and FixMyStreet contacts the council on your behalf.

It's run my **Mysociety.org**, a volunteer-based network who are behind a thriving set of websites promoting citizen rights. Their other sites include **TheyWorkForYou.com** (which will tell you exactly what your MP does on your behalf) and the **No 10 Petitions Website** (number10.gov.uk). Another, **WhatDoTheyKnow?** (whatdotheyknow.com), is possibly the most impressive of all. It makes it easy for you to log a freedom of information request to national or local government.

House Auction Bargains And Price-Drop Calculators

Is there a recession-specific way of buying a house? If there is, it's probably buying one at **auction**. **NethouseAuctions** (nethouseauctions.com) works with over three thousand estate agents and enjoys two million hits each day as people look to find a cheaper way of buying their new house.

You can search for the prices that houses have been sold for at auction in your local area (using their retrospective, postcode-based search at nethouseprices.com/index.php?con=Search-Sold-House-Prices), and you can certainly see that it's cheaper than the traditional market.

The opposite of the property ladder, according to this next particular website, is a property snake. **Propertysnake.co.uk** tracks information from

---

Landlords And Letting

From finding tenants to managing deposits, if you're a UK landlord then **Letting Zone** is the website for you. It was started in 2000 by Kent-based landlord Mark Garner and is full of helpful articles and blogs, like one on avoiding extortionate letting agent fees (lettingzone.com/landlord-legal-landlord-services/landlord-action-and-rent/477/using-a-letting-agent-and-the-Internet) by using Internet-based alternatives such as **Discount Letting** (discountletting.co.uk).

> ## Mortgage Calculators
>
> **Interactive Investor** has five calculator apps to help you figure your way
> through the mortgage maze. At iii.co.uk/mortgages/mortgage_calcs.jsp you'll
> find widgets to help you calculate your borrowing amount, **loan cost** (calculates
> monthly payments for a particular loan and interest rate), **loan savings** (cal-
> culates potential savings from remortgaging), and **flexible mortgage** (to see if
> flexible payment options might save you money). On the subject of calculators,
> **Money Back Mortgages** have an interesting widget on their site. As mentioned
> elsewhere in this chapter, they split the commission a mortgage broker would
> normally take for themselves 50/50 with you. And you can calculate what kind
> of cashback cheque that might entitle you to at moneybackmortgages.com/
> mortgageCashbackCalculator.php.

the main house-selling portals looking for the biggest discounts. On an average day, their database – which is updated daily – might have around 145,000
reduced prices, and reductions of up to, say, 55 percent.

Shopping Around For Your Mortgage

With your house found and price nailed, it's now time to enter the mortgage
world. Many of the **comparison sites** covered in Chapter 14 will help you
compare mortgage offers and repayments. And the **personal finance** and
advice sites in Chapter 19 also have a lot to offer borrowers. On the comparison front, moneysupermarket.com/mortgages is the main place to head
in the UK. The **Financial Services Authority** (FSA) also has a very easy to
understand mortgage comparison service at fsa.gov.uk/tables.

In the US, **Zillow.com** has a great system called **True Cost**. It's part of
the property site's **Mortgage Marketplace** and, as they explain, "is the only
mortgage shopping service that enables consumers to submit loan requests
anonymously and receive unlimited custom quotes from a network of thousands of confirmed lenders." Most importantly, all lenders who submit data
have to provide the full cost of their service, so Zillow.com's system will help
you avoid unexpected payments and penalties.

A less commercial, but equally useful, US site comes from Jack M.

Guttentag. He's an emeritus professor of finance at the Wharton School of the University of Pennsylvania and the self-styled "Mortgage Professor" (mtgprofessor.com). He has a huge amount of information, rates news and lender comparisons online and – very impressively – it's all categorized by who you are, as opposed to what you're looking for. So if you're in the US and you're a first-time home buyer, home seller, "elderly home owner mortgage shopper", or a "borrower with payment problems", or something completely different, studying with the Mortgage Professor is time worth investing.

Saving With An Online Mortgage

Another way to save money on your mortgage is to investigate the relatively embryonic world of **online-only mortgage brokers**. One example is **Email Mortgages** (who explain how their purely online system will save you paperwork and time at emailmortgages.com/theprocess.htm). Another, which will also give you some extra cash in your pocket, is **MoneyBackMortgages.com**, and their offering is very simple. You can either use their website to research the market and select your deal, or do it yourself using other sites – it makes no difference to them. Then, once you've selected your mortgage, you have three choices, as they outline at moneybackmortgages.com/howItWorks.php. The first is to apply direct to the lender. The second is to have a mortgage broker handle the paperwork and watch them accept a healthy commission from the lender. And the third is to use MoneyBackMortgages.com as your broker and, when they receive the commission, they'll split it with you 50/50.

Cutting Out The Middle-Man

Online estate agencies and **websites for private sales** are most definitely worth a look. How much could you save by using the web to circumnavigate estate agents? £4bn per year, according to the UK's **Land Registry**, who say that's how much UK estate agents take in fees between them. Ninety percent

Chapter 18

of house sales go through a traditional agent, but there's a lot of money to be saved if you join the ten percent minority.

The first step away from the High Street is to consider a web-only agent. "Online estate agents charge lower commission rates", says *The Guardian*'s Sally Hamilton, "such as **Halfapercent.com**, which typically charges an upfront fee of £199 plus 0.5 percent commission on completion, and **Hatched** (hatched.co.uk), which charges £398 for its most popular service." (Check her great step-by-step guide, *Selling a Home* at guardian.co.uk/money/2008/jun/19/property.houseprices.)

If you're selling in London, **Halfapercent.com** is a good bet. As they point out, 96 percent of London's house-hunters use the Internet so they market your property not only to an extensive database (almost fifty thousand buyers and tenants) but also through the main property portals I've already mentioned, such as **Rightmove** and **Primelocation** and also **Globrix Property Search** (globrix.com), **FindaProperty.com** and **PropertyLive.co.uk**.

Hatched makes a similarly compelling offering. Taking your details out to those same portals and 150 other websites, they reckon on getting it in front of eighty million buying searches each month. And the savings: Hatched say their customers save on average £3500!

Running in tandem with trad estate agents, and their online counterparts, are **housing ad sites**. These are cheaper still, although have a somewhat smaller audience reach. As you don't know what reaction you're going to get until you try, it could be worth placing an ad for your house on one of these sites first, just in case it sells. If you do get some interest from buyers, though, be prepared to handle all the estate agents' duties yourself, like arranging and facilitating viewings, and liaising with solicitors.

The Little House Company (thelittlehousecompany.co.uk) is the leading housing ad site. While online-only agents take a much smaller commission than their bricks and mortar counterparts, the likes of The Little House Company don't take a commission at all. All you pay is £89 to upload your details (or £135 for them to throw in some affiliate sites). Compared to giving £3000 (plus VAT) to a trad estate agent on a house sale of £200,000 … that's a mega saving. It's a bit like a paid-for version of **Gumtree** or **Craigslist** which, come to mention it, is the way to try and sell your house if you don't want to pay out any money at all!

House Price Crash Calculator

For some very depressing reading – or, perhaps, a chance to see if moving now is a good idea – check out the **House Price Crash Calculator** from **Thisismoney .co.uk**. "Enter the details of your property", they explain, "choose a year and see what would happen if prices crashed to the level they were then." It's at thisismoney.co.uk/house-price-crash-calculator.

Chapter 18

Repo Bargains?

As property expert Simon Shinerock points out, "**Repossessions** have attained an almost cult like status in the property world, so much so that to even dare to question the basis on which their status rests is tantamount to heresy." They certainly often come at a bargain price, can provide great rewards for developers, and are very attractive to first-time buyers. If it's an area that interests you, try Simon's detailed coverage of the repo market for **Propertyfinder.com** at propertyfinder.com/doc/third-party/choices/buying-repossessions.htm. There's also a free tutorial available to download on the subject at choices.co.uk/pfiTutorial.htm.

Two others to consider are **MyPropertyForSale** (mypropertyforsale.co.uk, one of the first "for sale by owner" websites dating back to 2001), and **Tepilo** (tepilo.com), a web venture by TV presenter Sarah Beeny (twitter.com/sarahbeeny).

Tepilo has a similar principle to The Little House Company but attempts to encompass all aspects of the buying process. They also, rather importantly, "host the negotiation process through the site (so) you are completely in control of how much (you) want to offer or accept on a home…" Find out more by browsing their advice pages for buyers and sellers at tepilo.com/buying_selling_advice/buying. Sarah and team's housing musings on Twitter are also worth checking out from time to time: twitter.com/tepilo.

19

Personal Finance

Financial Advice From The Online Surgery

Having looked at websites to help make savings across
different areas of our recession-conscious lives, there's
still a vast ocean of help and advice on the interweb that
applies across the board. So I've surfed, selected and loaded
the best into this chapter. And, save for the parting chapter
on freebie hunting, it seems logical to place this chapter at
the end of the book. Partly for all the people (like me) who
read most books from back to front. And partly because it
seems to mirror the broader, opening chapters on selling,
with some broader, closing chapters on economizing.

The objective here is to use the Internet to get the most out of your personal finances. From sites that track the best current account deals, budget
planners, tips on improving your credit rating, downloading template letters
for reclaiming bank charges, online calculators for you to figure out your

---

CheckFree

If there's a choice between dealing with a bank or business online or in real life, you'll sometimes get a little cash back in return for taking the online option. **Tiscali** (tiscali.co.uk) and **HSBC** (hsbc.co.uk), for example, both give you a token sum of money "back" in return for choosing web-, as opposed to paper-, based statements. And there's a site in the US that aims to combine all of your online bill-paying into one single interface, and gets the seal of approval from US News's **Alpha Consumer** columnist and money-saving guru Kimberly Palmer (usnews.com/blogs/alpha-consumer). **CheckFree** (MyCheckFree.com) obviously saves you time, money and the hassle of physically paying individual bills, but it also often saves you some money with businesses that offer incentives to pay online. They also have an emergency payment section, a kind of "express check-out", for people who suddenly find they're facing a late-payment penalty on a bill they've forgotten about and need to get it sorted PDQ.

---

state benefits and so on. Think of this chapter combined with your computer as your personal IFA (**Independent Financial Adviser**).

The Top Three

MoneySavingExpert

MoneySavingExpert (moneysavingexpert.com) is the brainchild of journalist Martin Lewis and is the kingpin of money-saving advice sites. Lewis isn't just the guru of consumer finance, he's a full-blown consumer rights activist, a full-on fiscal brainbox. There's a mountain of information on MoneySavingExpert (which can sometimes be its downfall) and I could spend a whole chapter listing what you might find. But it's easier to say that, if you're using the Internet to steer your frugal lifestyle, set MoneySavingExpert at the top of your top ten websites to check each day.

It all started in 2000 when Lewis used to regularly email money-saving tips to his friends. They would forward them to their friends and soon the word spread. In 2003 his website was launched and, by January 2009, it was receiving fifteen million hits every month. As the *Daily Mirror* once said (in its own *The Top 40 Money-Saving Websites* at mirror.co.uk/advice/money/2008/07/24/the-top-40-money-saving-websites-115875-20668928),

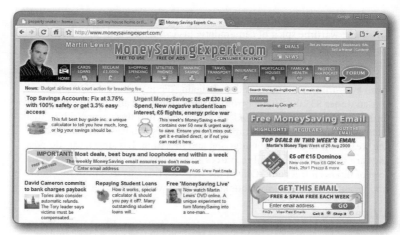

MoneySavingExpert is "the king of economy websites, it'll tell you how to do almost everything to save money. This site could save you thousands!" Or as **The Good Web Guide** (thegoodwebguide.co.uk) puts it, "Love him or hate him, Martin Lewis really knows his stuff when it comes to making the most of your money, and his comprehensive website reflects this."

The site is split up into ten key sections: **Credit Cards & Loans**, **Reclaim**, **Shopping & Spending**, **Utilities & Phones**, **Banking & Saving**, **Travel & Transport**, **Insurance**, **Mortgages & Houses**, **Family & Health**, and **Protect Your Pocket**. The latter covers all sorts of money-making and money-saving ventures, such as how to make money from online surveys and **The Demotivator Tool** ("Stops you spending when you can't afford it"). The Reclaim section is where more than six million UK residents have down-loaded **template letters** for claiming back unfair bank charges. The eleventh, and equally useful, section of the site is the forums, which draws hundreds of thousands of comments, questions and – unlike many such forums – is full of people willing to help you out and answer your questions.

GetRichSlowly.org

If there's one UK site you have to read on a near-daily basis it's **MoneySavingExpert**. And if there's one US site, it's **GetRichSlowly.org**. **CNN** declared it their "most inspiring money blog" and it's easy to see why. There's a simple chart of bank rates resident on the home page, a whole section

Chapter 19

devoted to getting out of debt (getrichslowly.org/blog/category/debt) and an almost wartime spirit of camaraderie (as evidenced with videos like this one: getrichslowly.org/blog/2009/07/25/buying-food-grocery-shopping-tips-from-1950).

Unlike MoneySavingExpert, the man behind GetRichSlowly.org has gone from everything to nothing and back again. "Four years ago, J.D. Roth was buried under $35,000 in debt from various consumer and home-equity loans and despaired of digging out", CNN explained when they awarded him their accolade. "Today the former cardboard-box salesman is debt-free and building wealth through careful budgeting and investing. His smart, can-do postings are stuffed with helpful resources and contagious enthusiasm about the joys of financial freedom." One of the websites that inspired both this book and its author, add it to your bookmarks forthwith.

Wise Bread

Wise Bread (wisebread.com) has a motto: "living large on a small budget". The site sets its aim on getting a little something extra for everything you buy, or getting something for nothing. So here you'll find articles like *How to Get Free Wi-Fi at Airports that Charge for Internet Connections* (wisebread.com/how-to-get-free-wi-fi-at-airports-that-charge-for-Internet-connections)

Online Tools

One of the best sites for online tools is **Money Matters To Me** (moneymatterstome.co.uk). Alongside family-oriented financial advice, they have very grapplable-with calculators for getting your head around loans, mortgages, repayments, savings and pensions.

---

and *Free Databases and Manuals at Public Libraries* (wisebread.com/free-databases-and-manuals-at-public-libraries). As *The New York Times* wrote in March 2009, "With the Dow below 7,000 right now, there may be a growing audience for Wise Bread's *Cornmeal: Fresh Ideas for a Frugal Family Staple* and its tips on removing car dents with a cigarette lighter, aluminium foil and an air duster." Wise Bread is US-centric, but so on-the-money when it comes to frugality tips and "life hacks" that it's worth browsing no matter where you're based.

Tips And Advice For Frugal Living

About.com & Crunchy Money

About.com, the Internet's original encyclopedia, has sections devoted to just about every area of modern life. Its frugality section (frugalliving.about .com) is written by an expert, Erin Huffstetler, who also writes the green living/green spending blog **Crunchy Money** (crunchymoney.com). You might find some of her articles, like her guide to *Edible Weeds* (frugalliving.about .com/od/eatforfree/tp/Edible_Weeds.htm), a little hard to stomach, but her step-by-step guide, *Create a Frugal Budget* (frugalliving.about.com/od/ frugalliving101/ht/Frugal_Budget.htm) is a vital piece of reading. It even reassures the most saving-averse readers with notes on how long the budget will take to put together.

Frugal Dad

Frugal Dad (frugaldad.com) comes from a slightly different perspective. It's another US site but one which works well in any language. As Jason White, the man behind it (and ex-financial call centre worker), points out, "it could be said that my advice is simply common sense." He's also supremely quali-

Chapter 19

Blogroll

There are no shortage of bloggers writing, ranting and theorizing their way through the credit crunch and their quest for a more frugal lifestyle. Here are just a few:

1 The Money Blog (blogs.thisismoney.co.uk/this_is_money_blog) Serious, journalistic, house-price-obsessed blog from the consumer finance specialists, **Thisismoney.co.uk**.

2 Living On A Dime (livingonadime.com/blog) Household tips and lots of reader interaction, from a mother and daughter team in Andover, Kansas.

3 Frugal For Life (frugalforlife.blogspot.com) Lots of news and detail from US blogger Dawn Cadwell, who was inspired to start her site after reading the late 1990s book *The Complete Tightwad Gazette* by Amy Dacyczyn. As she says on the site, "Thrift comes too late when you find it at the bottom of your purse."

4 Olivia Buck Needs Debt Help (blog.consumerchoices.co.uk/?author=180284) Devonian writer Olivia Buck's blog for **Consumer Choices** is a witty take on real-life attempts to save money.

5 MyColdwater.com Money Saving Blog (mycoldwater.wordpress.com) Another locally focused US site (for Coldwater, Michigan), but with some tips that translate across the country.

6 Money Saving Madness (moneysavingmadness.com) The work of a US mom obsessed with money-saving and discount coupons and vouchers, with the odd frugal living tip thrown in.

7 Consumerism Commentary (consumerismcommentary.com) A wealth, if you'll excuse the pun, of useful stories on banking, saving and investing (in the US) whose lead writer, Flexo, also dispenses pearls of wisdom on Twitter (twitter.com/flexo).

8 My 1st Million At 33 (1stmillionat33.com) Not the cheesy get-rich-quick site you might expect with such a name, this has lots of high-end advice and commentary on interest rates and stocks.

9 The Frugal Oenophile's Wine Of The Week (tfo-wow.blogspot.com) If all of this heavy reading leaves you in need of a drink, Canadian wine aficionado Richard Best writes this weekly wine review "on the basis of 'bang for the buck' ... I taste 100-200 wines each month hoping that I'll find at least a few that offer good, every day value."

---

fied from the "university of life"…

Frugal Dad's most popular articles are collected at frugaldad.com/best-of-frugal-dad/ and include *75 Money Saving Tips to Survive a Recession* (frugaldad.com/2008/06/16/75-tips-to-survive-a-down-economy), *How to*

Get Out of Credit Card Debt (frugaldad.com/2008/05/21/how-to-get-out-of-credit-card-debt-and-stay-out) and – one of the credos of this book – *The Difference in Being Frugal, and Being Cheap* (frugaldad.com/2008/03/26/the-difference-in-being-frugal-and-being-cheap/).

Google Tip Jar

In web terms, **Google Tip Jar** isn't particularly popular or well used, but it's a neat idea which – with the benefit of a few hundred thousand extra users – would be indispensable. It's based on the company's **Moderator app** (moderator.appspot.com), a simple conferencing service which lets people table and vote on motions, as they would do in a business meeting. To show how it works they've set up the **Tip Jar**, where you can suggest money-saving ideas and the rest of the moderator community can vote on how useful they are. The theory behind this "crowd-sourcing" app, as **Techcrunch** (techdreams.org/tips-tricks/5-best-websites-to-get-money-saving-tips/2025-20090326) describes it, is that as more people read the tips and vote on them, the most useful, helpful ideas will automatically ascend to the top of the list.

Frugal Village

Frugal Village (frugalvillage.com) is the work of prolific US journalist Sara Noel (whose other websites include **Homekeeping101.com** and **Budget Christmas.com**). Her theory is not dissimilar to that of Jason White at **Frugal Dad**, as her site claims that it "emphasizes simplicity, family values and eco-frugality." The best section to head for is the reader **Q&As**. It's full of those nagging little, mostly kitchen-related, questions that have always bugged me (and I thought it had always been *just* me). Like is it safe to put a warm chicken in the fridge, or should I leave it to cool first? And what's the best way to store bananas?

The Digerati Life

Savvy and sophisticated, **The Digerati Life** (thedigeratilife.com) is a blog by an anonymous ex-software developer known only as the **Silicon Valley Blogger**, or the **SVB**. She's prolific – as well as running this site you can catch her on the forums of the aforementioned **Wise Bread** (wisebread.com/silicon-valley-blogger) and running finance advice blog **The Smarter Wallet** (thesmarterwallet.com). In the absence of any major credit and debit card comparison websites in the US, the SVB comes to the rescue with guides

Chapter 19

such as *What Are the Best Credit Card Rewards Programs?* (thedigeratilife
.com/blog/index.php/2009/07/21/best-credit-card-rewards-programs) and
What's the Best Savings Account? (thedigeratilife.com/best-savings-account).

Wallet Pop

While all the other sites covered in this chapter so far are the work of one-
man and one-woman bands, there are a few corporate-backed financial websites that are worth looking at. **Wallet Pop** (walletpop.co.uk, and walletpop
.com in the US) comes from **AOL** and, in a bid to appeal to all and sundry, is
unsurprisingly celebrity-obsessed (so click to them for a chart of the richest
celebs under thirty, or to walletpop.co.uk/2009/03/16/when-celebs-fall-out-
of-favour-with-the-tax-man for a gallery of stars who have fallen foul of the
tax man). Their best advice comes as a combination of **economizing tips** and
stylish living, like their early-warning coverage of the **Hoxton Hotel £1 sale**
(hoxtonhotels.com/offers-1pound.php).

Lifehacker

There's almost too much information to cope with on **Lifehacker** (lifehacker
.com) but, the trouble is, it's almost all worth reading. Which makes for a
very addictive site. It's not just about saving money; Lifehacker's motto is "tips

and downloads for getting things done". One of their classic finds, the sort of thing Lifehacker is really useful for, is **Pantry**, a Windows and iPhone app from **ThinkFresher** (thinkfresher.com). "If you're looking for a way to keep track of what's on hand in your kitchen", Lifehacker's Erin Schwendemann explains, "with the option to share the list with others and sync it to your iPhone, Pantry may very well be your answer."

Zenhabits

From money-saving ideas to frugal living to life hacks ... There's a strange and steady path of transformation these websites seem to be taking us on. **Zenhabits** (zenhabits.net) takes things a little further. Yes, it has money-saving tips and, yes, it has ideas on how to live a more economy-proof lifestyle. But it will also lead with guides on subjects such as *Three Effective Ways to Enhance Your Willpower*. Does this warrant inclusion in this chapter? I definitely think so. After all, if I had better willpower, maybe I wouldn't have to spend so much time on MoneySavingExpert downloading budget calculators and saving spreadsheets.

I Will Teach You To Be Rich

Don't let the name of **I Will Teach You To Be Rich** (iwillteachyoutoberich. com) put you off. You might have similar concerns over a site with a name like this as with **My 1st Million At 33** (one of the blogs mentioned on p.180), but in the case of these two, your concerns would be unfounded. Admittedly coming from a slightly higher-handed tone than most, it's still worth browsing this work of author Ramit Sethi. His emphasis is on *automating* your savings and finances and it's a system that works. The flow chart at iwillteachyoutoberich.com/automating-your-money will give you an idea of where he's coming from. Or just watch him explain it on **YouTube** at youtube. com/watch?v=tE1s4Eg6SCE.

CashQuestions.com

There's a lot of reading available on the sites covered in this chapter. But who do you ask if you have a question? If it's a question on UK money or work, you could try the forums on **MoneySavingExpert**. And if it's a question on US affairs you could try Sara Noel Q&As at **Frugal Village**. If it's a question on **eBay** or **online shopping**, we'll come on to that at the end of this chapter. But for all other aspects of personal finance – from **student finance** to **"silver sav-**

ing" as they put it – try **CashQuestions.com**. It's run by three UK finance journalists and is headstrong and authoritative. It's free, too, and is the closest thing you'll find to an online IFA, your own web-based personal financial adviser.

Personal Shoppers And High Street Tips

Broke In The City

Broke In The City (twitter.com/brokeinthecity) is the Twitter page of a Canadian shopping addict who describes herself as "Just a girl trying to find a balance between being a **Shopaholic** and a **Saver** by living with less, but the best!" It's just the sort of Twitter feed that a desperate shopper needs to access while on the move: little sound bites to help you spot bargains and keep you motivated to avoid overspending. But the webpage it sprang from, **Fabulously Broke In The City** (fabulouslybroke.com) is an even better read, tracking one girl's hardcore budgeting from $60,000 of college debt to relative fluidity.

Show Me The Dough!

I knew **Show Me The Dough!** (savemoneyonfood.blogspot.com) had to be worth a look when US News' *Alpha Consumer* Kimberly Palmer described how it's run by "a mother of three who manages to keep her food bill under $300 each month, (who) offers savings tips as well as recipes". Though the site has since gone on hiatus, the recipes and advice it provides is pretty much guaranteed to make the raw ingredients in your cupboards stretch further.

Miss Thrifty

We may turn to bloggers, Twitterers and webmasters in times of financial stress, but there's a group of people who know a thing or two about economizing that we might easily overlook. And they're honoured in *Bowing to Frugal Grandma*, one of many wry pieces from **Miss Thrifty** (miss-thrifty .co.uk), a UK blogger who describes herself as a "label maven with a beady eye for bargains and a craving for saving." Like a UK version of **Broke In The City**, Miss Thrifty is the only frugal advisor tracking advice available on Twitter, and lists these as some of the most inspirational money-saving microbloggers:

Twitter.com/freefrombroke
Twitter.com/frugalbabe
Twitter.com/moneymatters
Twitter.com/moneycoach
Twitter.com/YouCanMakeThis

Chiconomise

All of the girly High Street money-saving sites like **Miss Thrifty** and **Broke In The City** provide info on the latest sales and discounts, but none with such determination as **Chiconomise** (chiconomise.com). "For the first time I watched *Confessions of a Shopaholic*", blogged the webmaster Ellie in summer 2009, "and I was faced with a grim reality. That was my life on screen…" So if you can't economize and you have to shop, then at least keep the spirit of bargain hunting, and if it's fashion, beauty and lifestyle stuff you're hording, this is the place to get some good deals.

Your Flexible F(r)iends

Credit card companies have a lot of information on file about you … it's a fact. So why shouldn't you have access to this information too? You might find some inaccuracies that are affecting your borrowing, or you might even spot identity theft. In the UK, **Experian** (experian.co.uk) and **Equifax** (equifax. co.uk) will both provide you with a free credit report, if you sign up to a thirty-day trial of their credit monitoring services. In the US, you'll find similar services from **myFICO** (myfico.com) – which will provide you with a report covering ninety percent of US banks and email alerts when your credit score changes – and at Experian's myfreecreditreport.com.

Once you've got your credit report, you might decide it's high time to save some money by **changing your credit card**. In which case, go to **Credit Card Searcher** (creditsearcher.co.uk) which provides up-to-date info on cards available, compared by key factors such as lowest standard rates, zero percent balance transfer deals and cashback/reward offers.

Better still is **Compareandsave.com** which, in July 2009, launched not one but four interactive calculators to help you find the **best credit card deals**. "Each calculator will help consumers to answer some of the common questions they are likely to encounter when using or comparing credit cards", they explain, "especially when they are looking for the best balance transfer offers or other ways to save money on their credit card bills. Other answers the new credit card tools will provide are how long it will take to pay off a credit card balance and at what cost if consumers only make minimum repayments." Compareandsave.com's four calculators are all must-bookmark tools for the online saver…

1 The Balance Transfer vs Low Rate Credit Card Calculator (compareandsave .com/tools/calculators/credit-card-calculators/balance-transfer-vs-low-rate-credit-card-calculator) This will help you find out if you'll save most by going for either a zero percent balance transfer or a low-rate card.

2 The Minimum Repayment Credit Card Calculator (compareandsave.com/ tools/calculators/credit-card-calculators/minimum-repayment-credit-card-calculator). This one will show you how much longer you're going to be tied in, and how much extra money you'll have to pay, if you only make the minimum payments each month on your credit card bill. Scary stuff!

3 The Credit Card Payoff Calculator (compareandsave.com/tools/calculators/ credit-card-calculators/credit-card-payoff-calculator) This tool simply shows you how long it will take you to pay off your credit card debts.

4 The Balance Transfer Calculator (compareandsave.com/tools/calculators/balance-transfer-calculator) And finally, this one is handy if you've got a zero percent balance transfer deal in mind – it shows you how much money you might save, based on current debts and interest rates.

New Money Marketplaces

All of the websites in this chapter offer advice on traditional money markets. But there are other, emerging ways of handling your finances that are appearing online. In the UK **Zopa** (zopa.com) is a prime example. It's a website that provides a platform for "social lending" which means, at the simplest level, that you can use it to lend money to other people and earn some interest, or to borrow money and circumnavigate the banks to pay less interest than you might elsewhere. For a similar US site, try **Prosper.com**. As **MSN Money** (money.msn.com) explains, "By cutting out the bank middlemen and many of the overheads, borrowers get lower rates and lenders get higher ones."

Zopa beat off the likes of its competitor **Lending Club** (lendingclub.com) and advice site **Mint.com** to win the **Webby Award** (webbyawards.com) for *Best Financial Services Website* in 2008. But its most important recognition came from the **Retail Banker International Global Awards** where it fended off **PayPal** to win *Most Threatening Non-Bank Competitor*.

Chapter 19

From a lender's perspective, you get the chance to invest some money and see it benefit other people, as opposed to watching it slosh around a faceless business. "Lending at Zopa felt different", reports one user profiled on uk.zopa.com/ZopaWeb/public/about-zopa/who-uses-zopa.html. "It's really easy to use – and I found myself a little more involved – looking regularly to see who I had lent to. I've also been really pleased to see how stringently Zopa vets borrowers. They don't allow my money to be lent to just anyone, and this gives me great confidence."

Like lenders, borrowers are also in somewhat unchartered territory with a system like this, but Zopa is not short on firm backers and financial credentials. "The borrowing process was so easy", reports Rebecca, one of their flagship users. "I loathe banks. It makes me very angry how much gets creamed off any product and it rocks me to my soul how much I spend on interest … it feels so greedy." Zopa is available in the UK (uk.zopa.com), US (us.zopa.com), Japan and Italy.

Here's another different take on things. If you're borrowing from a traditional bank, how about having them all queue up to give you the best interest rate and actually bid for your business, rather than the other way round? This is the theory behind **Licuro.com**, which launched in the UK in July 2009, having spun off from its established Danish counterpart, **Mybanker.biz**.

"British households saved 4.8 percent in the first quarter of 2009", explains Licuro.com's founder John Norden, "(yet) interest rates for savers are still risibly low. So it's a good time to be launching an online interest rate auction house that gives savers (individuals, companies and organizations) the chance to lend their cash to the highest bidder. We've proven through our operations in Europe that the interest rates banks are prepared to offer via auction are materially higher than the rates offered both on the High Street and on ordinary online savings sites so it makes sense for savers."

There's a sign-up fee involved (£5.75 for one transaction, or £33.35 for a year) and from then you just register how much you plan to save (or, as Licuro.com puts it, how much you want to lend the banks) and you'll get your offers back within a couple of hours.

Quite how this self-styled "eBay for savers" works out remains to be seen. But it's certainly succeeded in Denmark. Established in 2002, Mybanker.biz works with 23 Scandinavian banks and, in the first six months of 2009, eight thousand savers deposited £2.2 billion through the site.

Mylostaccount.org.uk

You may be thinking about saving money and living the frugal life in times of recession, but maybe it hasn't always been so. Maybe you have some money in a bank account from years ago that you've completely forgotten about which, if tracked down, could provide a nice little windfall? This is not as over-optimistic as you might think. It's estimated that there's over £850 million sloshing around across half a million lost, dormant or forgotten bank accounts in the UK alone. So you could do worse then spending a few minutes making sure that some of this mega total isn't yours. **Mylostaccount.org** was set up in 2008 by the **British Bankers' Association** together with the **Building Societies Association** and **NS&I** and it carries out hundreds of thousands of free searches each year. You can enter all your details (and carry out your claim, if you find a lost account) through their website and they have a useful set of FAQs at mylostaccount.org.uk/help.htm.

Serious Advice...

Here's a final rampage through a dozen more personal finance websites, less focused on economizing and more on finding the best financial products in the quagmire of conflicting messages and ramped-up recession-specific advertising from the banks...

1 Moneyspider.com takes the details of your trust and fund investments and provides you with a daily report on their performance and their earning potential.

2 Moneyexpert.com Part comparison site, part advice portal, Moneyexpert .com is great for finding the best deals on mortgages and credit cards. They also have a telephone help line.

3 Moneymagpie (moneymagpie.com) is the work of TV presenter Jasmine Birtles and, among much else, has a very useful introductory guide to Child Trust Funds (moneymagpie.com/article/781/child-trust-funds-ctfs-free-money-for-your-children).

4 Money.co.uk is a clear and authoritative comparison site (comparing almost seven thousand personal finance products from over seven hundred companies) but is flagged up in this chapter, rather than Chapter twelve, for its useful guides, like this one on the pros and cons of "package current accounts": money.co.uk/article/1004147-are-package-current-accounts-worth-the-cost.htm.

Chapter 19

Official Help

It has to be said that the government websites for helping you out of a financial crisis – on both sides of the pond – are really useful. In the US, **Hud.gov**, the home of the US **Department of Housing and Urban Development**, is a good place to start. And in the UK, the **Citizens Advice Bureau** website is fantastic: clear, easy to read and full of advice on all aspects of modern living, not just finance.

---

5 Moneynet.co.uk has been praised by the *Daily Mirror*'s Alison Palmer as it "compares mortgages to suit all needs from those buying for the first time to those remortgaging, finding it hard to get a mortgage or buying-to-let." But I'm including it in this round-up for its *Tip of the Week.* They're almost always thought-provoking and you can read an archive of them at moneynet .co.uk/Personal-Finance-News/Tips.

6 Blogging Banks Courtesy of *Recession Wire*: "Blogging Banks (bloggingbanks.com) tracks bank offers", they report, and "Bank Deals (bankdeals.blogspot.com) has daily and weekly updates on interest rates."

7 AllAboutLoans.co.uk This site is a trad, comparison-based alternative to Zopa. You just type in the amount you'd like to borrow, your preferred APR and it will come back with results from the key lenders for you to weigh up.

8 FinancialAdvice.co.uk This one is like an online newspaper of news across finance, politics and the intersection of the two.

Advice For eBayers

To get the most out of any website you need to talk to people – online or offline – to share tips and ideas. The way to do this on **eBay** is through the "Community Centre" at hub.ebay.com/community. It's the official home to the feedback system and the place to meet and talk to other users in departments such as **Discussion Boards**, **Groups**, **Answer Centre** and **Chat Rooms**.

Discussion Boards

There are over a hundred discussion boards on eBay (pages.ebay.com/ community/boards), all of which vary wildly in usefulness. And friendliness! The best ones to start with are the **General Discussion Boards** and its

New To eBay section. It's full of people willing to answer even the simplest of questions, which can be very handy given the slow response times of eBay's official help lines. It's best to browse the others – most of which have kooky names like *The Front Porch* (for general chatting with other buyers and sellers), *The Homestead* (on house-related subjects), *The Park* (recreation), *The Soapbox* and so on – and see which subjects or threads take your interest. It's a very US-centric part of the site but the *eBay Friends From All Over* forum seeks to address that.

If you are only really interested in one particular area of buying and selling – such as cars, shoes or watches – the fifty or so category-specific discussion boards can be very useful. Each receives about a dozen new topics each day. Those who buy and sell frequently should try the **Community Help Boards**. These self-help groups are categorized by the main hurdles of everyday eBaying, like photos, searching, feedback and **PayPal**.

The Chatter is eBay's official newsletter and provides lots of connections to other users. It's been running since November 2002 and can be found at pages.ebay.com/community/chatter. You can email nino@ebay.com to receive advance warning of new editions. It's also home to *Ask Griff*, where users can pose questions to eBay's "in-house guru", Jim Griffith.

Chapter 19

Groups

eBay's **Groups** (groups.ebay.com) are friendlier and less business-focused forums, where users get together to discuss a common interest, or just because they happen to be in the same country or region. There are almost one thousand **Collectors Club** groups, with clothing, toys and cards being the most popular. And there are almost as many **Special Interest Groups** – a variation on the same theme – to choose from. They're certainly a diverse bunch, ranging from the useful *(Shopping For Baby On Ebay)* to the niche *(Acoustic Music)* to the plain bizarre (*Bromeliadhead* – they're crazy about epiphytes).

To connect with other eBayers near you, try the **Regional Interest Groups**. There are over a hundred, largely focused on the US, with the regions in question being mainly individual US states, though there's a brace of international groups accommodating various countries who are yet to receive their own localized version of the website itself. These regional groups are also where **eBay Singles** gather together, as do the **Witches of New England** or the more straightforward **Philippine PowerSellers**. Unlike the rest of the site, which is based on categories within categories, eBay's community section is chaotic and sprawling.

If the thousands of forums and meeting places on eBay fail to connect you with someone or something meaningful, answer your question or improve your selling and saving, it's very easy to create your own. You need a minimum feedback score of fifty and to have been a member for at least ninety days. Go to **Community > Groups > News & Events** to get started.

Or you could hire a **mentor**. eBay's mentoring system has 27 individual forums covering **Buying**, **Selling** and **One Time Help**. Mentoring is something eBay has started to encourage of its best users – those with 99 percent positive feedback, a total feedback score higher than 50 and members of the eBay volunteers programme. Go to **Home > Community > Groups > eBay Volunteers Program** to find out more. Many of the mentors run discussion groups, with the most popular being *The Business Side of eBay Selling* and *A. Cherbear's Help with HTML & Descriptions*.

Answer Centre

If there's an area of eBaying that has you stumped, the **Answer Centre** (pages. ebay.com/community/answercenter) is the place to head. Easily the most useful part of all the Community section, the Answer Centre is a thriving,

---

eBay From Outside In

It's always a good idea to chat about eBay and meet other users independently of the site itself, so here are five popular forums worth investigating.

1 Antique-shop.com antique-shop.com/forums

2 AuctionBytes auctionbytes.com/forum/phpBB

3 AuctionHints auctionhints.com/message

4 AuctionSniper community.auctionsniper.com

5 Vendio vendio.com/mesg

---

searchable Q&A forum. You simply post a question to the relevant area and other eBayers queue up to answer and help out. All of the answers are published beneath your original question, giving you a second and third opinion. And you can also browse and search on previous questions, which might save you posting in the first place. All of the obvious subjects are covered, like **bidding**, **PayPal**, **searching**, and **Stores**, along with equally useful sections devoted to **trading**, **technical issues**, **insurance** and so on.

Click on **Miscellaneous** to share in other eBayers' mid-sale worries too, like "what do I do if he doesn't pay?", "what should I do about this unconfirmed address?" and "what does the number beside a user ID mean?"

Chat Rooms

The least useful – and least friendly – part of eBay's Community, the **Chat Rooms** (pages.ebay.com/community/chat), are rough and ready and full of cliquey in-jokes and shouting. Certainly not the place for beginners, or anyone after serious (or even particularly witty) conversation. If you have a special interest you would be far better served in a group rather than chat room. But what you'll find here is conversations set out in one long continuous stream of messages, as opposed to being grouped by subject, question or even thread. There are a dozen general chat rooms to choose from, starting with the first ever to be set up, the **eBay Café**.

Have a look at pages.ebay.com/university/instructors.html and you'll see the fourteen tutors who spend their time delivering in-person eBay **training sessions** around North America. Would you like to spend a day in a room with these people? If the answer is yes, and you prefer to learn the finer points of eBay face to face, then you can sign up for their so-called

Chapter 19

eBay University. They currently cover a dozen US cities and Toronto and Vancouver in Canada too, offering a full-day session either on *Selling Basics* or *Beyond the Basics*. No instructors are presently available in Europe or the rest of the world, but you can access their courses on the Internet, DVD or CD-Rom.

eBay Live!

eBay Live! (pages.ebay.com/eBayLive), meanwhile, is the website's annual gathering of sellers, developers and browsers – in fact, anyone and everyone that's involved in the eBay experience. A freaky cross between a giant garage sale and a political convention, it takes place over three days when ten thousand users and hundreds of exhibitors converge on one hotel, Mandalay Bay in Las Vegas being 2006's venue. It certainly takes the face-to-face experience a stage further, with speed networking and some educational sessions being truly useful. But you have to balance this with the prospect of self-congratulatory speeches from eBay executives and – the entertainment for 2005's event

Shoppers Anonymous

From advice on **eBay buying and selling** to advice on **eBay addiction** – it does happen, and can creep up on you when you're least expecting! eBay themselves don't help the addicts, they just spur them on with that classic "don't let this item get away!" email you automatically receive when you've been outbid. But addiction happens to all of us.

One tell-tale sign of addiction is too many late nights at the screen. You go online to check a bid and realize you've been there for hours, searching for those unusual shower hooks.

If you really are worried about your buying habits, you can try the **Centre for Online Addictions** which was founded in 1995 and offers therapy specifically for eBay users at netaddiction.com/resources/auction_houses.htm. Or try this great checklist from humour portal flipsided.com, to find out if you're an addict…

1 Every time you go to the grocery store, you offer the cashier one cent more for each item in the cart of the person in front of you.

2 You set your alarm clock for 3am so you can log on to protect your bid.

3 You've sworn at the screen when someone's outbid you at the last second.

4 You've questioned your sanity because of the price you've bid … more than once.

5 You've rolled your eyes at the word "antique" or "vintage" used on something made in the past decade.

6 You've bid on something even though the picture doesn't show up correctly.

7 You've changed all your clocks to "eBay official time (PDT)".

8 You've made My eBay your default home page.

9 After a particularly passionate night, you lean over and whisper in your spouse's ear, "Excellent service, great communication! Would recommend again! AAAA++++"

10 Sitting on the floor of your empty apartment, you stare at your fingers and wonder whether they'll sell better individually or as a matched set.

– a performance by **Weird Al Yankovic**. You can find out more at pages.ebay.com/ebaylive but users' own convention blogs like ebaynews.blogs.com and phoons.com/john/ebaylive2005 give much more of an insight.

20

Sites For Freebies

Voucher Codes, Coupons, Swap Sites And Cashback

Getting something for nothing is too lofty a dream. But, if you're buying anything online, there's an increasing array of websites tracking discounts and special offers that will save you money. The stores don't always like them. They prefer to promote their special deals just to select customers. But it takes just one person to blog about, for example, an electrical store offering free shipping if you enter a certain code when you buy online, and the message spreads like wildfire.

Sites that repromote – and make their living – from spreading the word about special deals have come under fire from retailers. And there are a few examples where certain, highly targeted discounts have cost online stores a small fortune once the world at large found out. But us consumers have nothing to feel guilty about. If you find a discount code – no matter what the source – that works when you make your online purchase, go for it. The onus is on the store, not us, to make sure **promotions, deals and discounts** are managed correctly.

Get Money Off...

I'm talking about a whole set of things under one banner here. **Discount codes**, namely the little codes you get to enter just as you click "Buy" in an online store that might entitle you to a discount, free shipping or giftwrapping. Then there's **discount vouchers** – more commonly referred to as **coupons** if you're in the US – which you print out and take to a bricks and mortar store (or restaurant, or wherever) to hand over in exchange for money off, or a free dessert, etc.

It's worth noting that it's often quite easy to find out about the best deals on the virtual grapevine. So keep your ear to the ground on **Twitter**, **Facebook** and **forums** where people often send out messages such as *"just printed off a great two-for-one voucher to use at Joe's Pizza. Get it for yourself at http://blah.blah..."*

An even easier way of checking for discount codes is **Google**, of course. It makes total sense to keep up to date on the dedicated voucher sites but, if you have a particular purchase in mind (a Samsung flatscreen TV, for example), then it's a no-brainer to Google for **Samsung + TV + discount + code** before you start surfing and comparison shopping to find the best price.

Reader Feedback At Moneysavingexpert.com

The best place for getting regular updates on UK deals and discounts is the **MoneySavingExpert.com** website. Make your first port of call their **Top Deals** page at moneysavingexpert.com/deals/discount-voucher-codes. Here you'll find some very tempting offers – and info on how to obtain them – like *"£5 off a £30 spend at Lidl"*, *"20% off any purchase at Oasis"*, and so on. These are compiled by the site's research team but also rely heavily on reader recommendations, submitted via the **Discount Vouchers Discussion** section of their forum at forums.moneysavingexpert.com.

The good thing about this forum – and all other non-commercial voucher sites – is that you can find out what other shoppers think about the deals before you try them out for yourself.

Do Coupon Sites Really Work?

The answer to this is a resounding YES. They really can save you significant amounts of money. In the US, **Coupon Cabin**'s users have downloaded over 150 million vouchers since they opened their doors in 2003 and their average user saves $16 on every purchase they make. In the UK, **MyVoucherCodes** reports that – in 2008 alone – its five hundred thousand users made 2.5 million purchases and generated £28 million in savings for themselves.

Coupon Sites In The US

In the US there's a veritable industry based around websites collecting, categorizing and promoting **discount coupons,** both the sort you print out to take to a store and those you enter online. By far the easiest to use, most well laid out, and certainly one of the most well stocked, is **RetailMeNot.com**. They have ninety thousand coupons in their searchable database, with typical deals along the lines of *"free shipping on orders over $75 at Urban Outfitters"*. They've also got some nice spin-off apps like **Hot Coupons 1.0**, a Mac **Dashboard Widget** (apple.com/downloads/dashboard/shopping/hotcoupons.html) and an **iGoogle Gadget**.

Hot Coupon World comes second to RetailMeNot.com with sixty thousand coupons online. But they do have a load of tip-tastic instructional videos at hotcouponworld.com/hotcouponworld-on-youtube.

Also worth searching, especially if you're on the cusp of a major purchase, are **Alex's Coupons** (alexscoupons.com, which covers 1200 online stores), **Coupon Cabin** (couponcabin.com), **CouponCode.com** (with big brand stores like **Sears** and **Macy's**), and **Coupon Mountain** (couponmountain.com, which claims to cover five thousand online stores). Finally, if you're a regular **Amazon** and **Buy.com** shopper, you'll find all the latest discount codes for both sites filed away at **RefundsPlease.com**.

Freeshipping.org

All of the deals on the US coupon sites can be quite overwhelming. So one simple page to add to your favourites is this, **Freeshipping.org**. It holds coupons for more than 1500 online stores including **eBay**, **Gap** and **Macy's**. So if you're about to make a purchase, check here before you click on "Confirm Order" and you'll probably have your item sent to you for nothing,

US Groceries

One of the biggest areas you can save money on with US coupon sites is your grocery bill. The biggest and best website for doing so is **TheCouponClippers** (thecouponclippers.com) which claims to save shoppers at least twenty to thirty percent off their weekly grocery bills, and has the stats and credentials to back this up. But the site is dense and not for the newbie, who would be better suited to stuffing their grocery purse with deals printed off from the **Penny Pincher Gazette** (ppgazette.com). Two other characters who can reduce your food bill are **CouponMom.com** and a blogger called **MoneySavingMom.com**.

Voucher Codes In The UK

In the UK, the whole coupon thing is lagging somewhat behind the US side of the web. But there are still some good sites out there, and some really decent discounts and bargains to be had. **Hotukdeals** (hotukdeals.com) has none of the adverts that cover such US sites, and comes from an underground spirit of consumer activism. Their motto? "Deal anarchy from the masses."

Certainly the most authoritative UK voucher site is **MyVoucherCodes .co.uk**. It's ad-free, continually updated and covers all the main High Street brands. Coming a close second is the dense, category-based **Codes.co.uk**. For grocery savings, **FixtureFerrets.co.uk** saves most of its users at least £10 off their regular online shop, but does charge a subscription fee for access to its most up-to-date deals.

Money For Your Old Music, Books And Bling

If you're not selling off your unwanted or surplus CDs on **eBay** (see p.38) and **Amazon** (see p.60), and not passing them on with **Freecycle** (see p.93), then **Musicmagpie.co.uk** will take them off your hands for a relatively low, but not-to-be-sniffed-at, rate. Having been running for fewer than five years they've already paid out close to £2 million for second-hand CDs – and

also DVDs and games – sent in by users (and you can see this total increase live at musicmagpie.co.uk/general_info.asp). An equivalent site in the US is **Abundatrade.com** which pays out for your old books, too.

And what about bling? Well, according to **YourGoldForCash.co.uk**, "the price of gold has increased by 171 percent in the last five years and the combination of high demand and weaker sterling have pushed the price of gold to record highs", so they're busy hoovering up and paying out on unwanted (and broken) gold jewellery gathering dust in drawers and wardrobes around the UK. They provide a full valuation pack free of charge, and paid out £25,000 in the first two months after they launched. In the US, the best site to try is **Cash4Gold.com**.

Cashback Sites

Getting a little bit of money back every time you make a purchase has a very tempting ring to it. And it's possible, thanks to a new breed of **cashback sites**. How do they work? It's simple. All of the major web shops normally pay a referral fee to "affiliate" sites that send them customers. So if you click over to a supermarket via an ISP portal, for example, the ISP gets a token fee when you make a purchase. What cashback sites do is pass that referral fee straight back to you. Everyone's a winner, or at least that's the theory.

Like the coupon sites, these cashback sites work best if you have your heart set on a new purchase, rather than for general browsers. If you've decided on a new PC from **PC World**, for example, or something for the garden from **Argos**, then – rather than clicking direct to the retailers' own sites – it makes perfect sense to set up an account with a cashback site, access PC World or Argos via them, and pocket the referral fee.

Chapter 20

UK Cashback Sites

Quidco (quidco.com) is a good place to start and they charge just £5 per year (which is taken from your cashback earnings; you don't have to pay it direct). **Give Or Take** (giveortake.com) works on the same principle. It costs £25, but also raises money for charity, as well as your bank balance. **Rpoints** (rpoints .com) charges £5 per month and has a healthy stack of satisfied customers singing its praises.

One typical punter said that "Over the last six months I have earned £550 in cashback", and, just as impressively, this was "Just from purchases I would have made anyway..." But perhaps the best way to dip a toe in the water of cashback sites is with one that doesn't charge anything to take part. For this, head to **Kelkoo**'s cashback.kelkoo.co.uk, which has no sign-up fee and links to six hundred High Street brands including **Argos**, **ASDA**, **Tesco** and **Currys**.

Getting Your Dues

State benefits aren't what you'd call freebies, but there are websites out there to help make sure you're getting what's due to you. According to **Entitledto** (entitledto.co.uk), "People across the UK are missing out on benefits and tax credits worth more than £10 billion a year". Their site has a simple calculator which you can use to find out if you are missing out on any rightful financial assistance. The **Citizens Advice Bureau** also has a very detailed webpage listing all types of benefits currently available in the UK at adviceguide.org.uk/index/life/benefits.htm. Once you've made sure you know what you're entitled to, check you haven't been overpaying on High street banks' overdraft charges and penalty fees. Click through a simple process to find out if you're owed anything – and claim it back – on the **Home Advisory Service** website at homeadvisoryservice.co.uk/reclaim_bank_charges.asp.

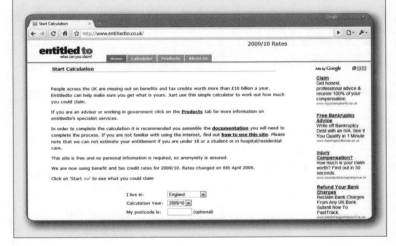

US Cashback Sites

In the US, **Ebates** (ebates.com) is the one to go for. It's been running since 1999 and, in that time, has sent cashback payments to its members totalling over $40 million, yes, million... **Microsoft** also has its own cashback system in the US, at bing.com/cashback.

Chapter 20

Don't Pay For It, Swap For It

There is one way of getting the goods you need not for a ten percent voucher discount, but for a one hundred percent thrift discount. Swap for it. In the US, if you have **books** or **DVDs** that you want to get hold of – and have a stack of similar items that you can't be bothered to sell (or that you know would fetch next to nothing) – you can set up a swap at **Eswapnow.com**. In the UK, the most popular swap site is **Read It Swap It** (readitswapit.co.uk), which is sitting on a library of almost three hundred thousand books from its user base.

Swap sites can really help you save a lot of money, as swaps are based not on equivalent monetary value, but on one-to-one wish lists. So say I have a VHS copy of *Moonraker* to swap (not that I'd ever dream of getting rid of

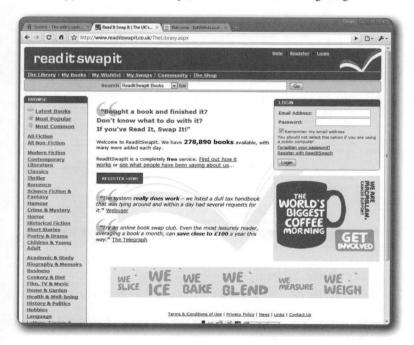

such a Bond/cheese classic). This might only fetch a few pence on **Amazon Marketplace** now that the world has moved to DVD. But I might find a user on a swap site that really wants this particular video tape, who would be willing to swap for something I really want too … perhaps with a much higher monetary value.

Free Eats And Tickets

Ah, we've arrived at the last selection of money-saving websites in this whole book. Which means you and I should head out for a cut-price meal and maybe some entertainment, to celebrate this journey into post-credit crunch frugal living. First up, make your **restaurant booking** through either **Toptable** (toptable.com) or **5pm** (5pm.co.uk). Both give you reward points

towards free meals each time you make a booking. You get 200 points when you sign up to Toptable, two hundred more each time you make a reservation and, at 1400 points, a free meal out.

Another website for arranging a meal out at zero cost, and maximum interest, is **Eatwithalocal.com**. It's a social networking site where people upload their tastes for food and cooking and, when you're in their area, you can arrange to pop round and meet them for a meal.

After food, the night out with the highest glamour to lowest cost ratio has to be tickets to see a TV show being recorded. That's because they're always given out free and – as always – you just need to know the right websites to go to to collect them. In this case, we're talking **ApplauseStore.com** and **SRO Audiences** (sroaudiences.com).

Part 5: Index

Index

Index

Index

Index

Index

Index

Index

Sites You've Found: